ON-A

INNOVATION-ARCHITECTURE

INNOVATION AT **ON-A** ARCHITECTURE

By Ricardo Devesa

ON-A'S VALUES

ON-A's founding partners (Eduardo Gutiérrez and Jordi Fernández) have always oriented their professional practice toward the constant pursuit of innovative and ad hoc solutions for every project. They have relied on cutting-edge technologies and ongoing research into advanced design tools, in the service of the most avant-garde yet at the same time humanistic ideas. Since the very beginning, research has been their leitmotif. A recurring theme, part of their idiosyncrasy. That attitude extends to their team at large and their external collaborators.

The fundamental values of ON-A's work can be described as innovation in terms of:

1_ experimentation using complex geometries with the ability to address multiple demands at the same time, by encoding parameters (**Design**),
2_ sustainability, seeking out advanced bioclimatic solutions (**Sustainability**),
3_ improving inhabitants' quality of life, by offering more comfortable and also exciting environments (**Emotion**),
4_ and a continual improvement of construction techniques and materials that increase efficiency in all areas (**Technology**).

ON-A's designs are recognized for seeking out bold and intelligent solutions that offer concrete measures to respond to the myriad requirements of any architectural design, including meeting environmental challenges, implementing technological innovations, offering integrative and surprising design solutions, and creating spaces for connection with nature and the surroundings.

Research is a constant for the firm in the construction of their designs, as well as in the commissioning process, and with regard to profitability and maintenance.

Each ON-A project is an opportunity to experiment with new spatial and material models; to maximize efficiency and sustainability throughout the project's life cycle; and to establish a respectful coexistence between society and the environment.

Another of ON-A's noteworthy values is engaging with and responding to the challenges facing today's cities and the cities of the near future. Challenges that include the climate crisis, the efficiency of natural resources and, currently, the dilemmas brought about by the public health crisis. Those responses include, for example, incorporating greenery as an active agent in the construction of architectural spaces, at all scales, improving today's urban conditions by generating healthier ones; reconnecting people with the natural biological environment, and thus supporting more balanced ecosystems.

The Smart Mesh Building in Taipei was developed based on parametric design innovations. **--See page 44--**

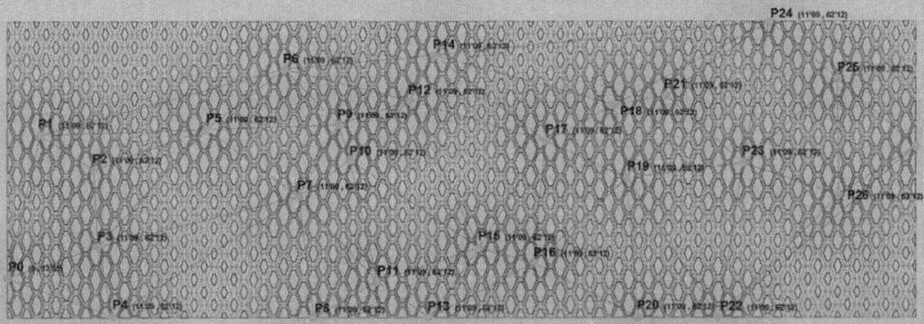

The innovation of the building is its façade, composed of a double skin formed from rhomboid elements that are adapted, with different-sized openings, depending on the orientation and sun exposure.

Model of the building at night, it shines like a geometric lantern in the middle of the city.

NEW PARADIGMS, NEW RESPONSES

ON-A has aimed to be one of the forerunners in a new architectural and urban paradigm, providing new responses based, for instance, on bio-construction and energy self-sufficiency (Sustainability); based on formalization and creativity to resolve complex requirements comprehensively (Design); based on a commitment to creating pleasant environments and memorable experiences for inhabitants (Emotion); and based on originality in the use of the ensemble of material components and their effective installation during construction (Technology).

They understand urbanism and architecture from a perspective of social and environmental responsibility. Their designs

The Bio-tech Tower facade, a large structural mesh, allows a large glazed surface so that all rooms are connected to the outside.
--See page 130--

and constructions advocate a commitment to mitigating the negative effects of traditional construction, which consumes already scarce natural resources and has a significant impact on the global economy. In response, they incorporate the management and optimization of the use of water, sun or wind in their urban proposals. Or they introduce the combination of technology and ecology to create sustainable, wholesome and healthy spaces.

For ON-A, a respect for nature is essential in architecture. They use non-polluting materials, optimized energy sources and renewable resources; they improve air purification, condition each environment in which they build climatologically; they establish an optimum visual relationship with the natural environment and thus generate a sensation of calm and environmental comfort. They contribute to improving the environment and creating healthier and more emotional spaces for people and other species, helping to incite emotion and an appreciation for what is alive in their buildings' users (a concept known as "biophilia", used for the first time by the psychologist and philosopher Erich Fromm, in 1973, to refer to the "love of life").

In that sense, they understand each design as a catalyst for positive emotions. They offer the inhabitants physical-visual wellbeing. They generate an interior comfort that contributes to the occupants' vitality. Incorporating emotion into technology helps them act responsibly towards the environment and, at the same time, towards the inhabitants – as they explained in their first book entitled *ON-A: Emotion-Architecture (Artpower, 2014).*

For ON-A, technology is a key tool for promoting design, creativity and responsibility. For this reason, they carry out complete models of their projects (functional, structural, building services, and maintenance), which gives them full control over every design phase. The management of ON-A's buildings is formulated from the initial design all the way through to conservation. They manage all the information in the form of data through the building models. This method lets them visualize and interact with the continuum of information and workflows during all phases of the project.

Investment in R&D has allowed ON-A to develop their own technical know-how, which guarantees high performance in real time when it comes to the evolution and transformation of designs, taking into account the entire life cycle of the project; this is a key factor in achieving a positive, optimized impact on the energy consumption of their buildings.

ON-A addresses the emerging paradigms by using innovation in new forms of planning, building, and relating with the natural environment; by investigating other possible scenarios in the organization of society and the environment; and by experimenting with technologies applied to sustainable proposals to introduce new approaches, strategies, and relationships between the city, architecture and its inhabitants.

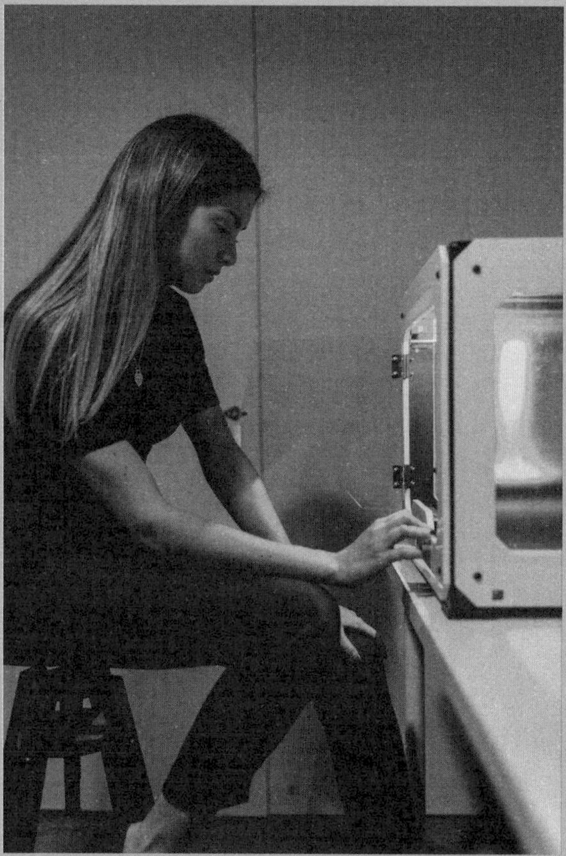

ON-A means "on-architects" in the sense of we awake, alert, active, and always search new ways to innovate.

A MULTIDISCIPLINARY TEAM

Since its foundation in 2005, ON-A has operated as a creative and multidisciplinary team capable of approaching each project in a unique and personalized way. After 15 plus years, they continue to develop and build innovative and compelling works and designs in their laboratory, rooted in experimentation, sustainability and efficiency, as well as excellence in architectural and urban design.

The ON-A's laboratory and showroom in Barcelona, is a platform that encourages the research and development of new technologies and working methods in the field of architecture and construction.

ON-A is associated with a lineage of practices that are disruptive within the discipline of architecture, but without falling into the formalism or iconicity of some of the figures of the late 20th and early 21st centuries. The collaborations and synergies between the different specialties of each of their collaborators and professionals help them to achieve excellence while implementing R&D, BIM management tools, bio-construction and the application of new materials and construction systems in all their projects.

The team takes part in continuing professional development to ensure they remain at the forefront of the latest knowledge and practices in all areas of architecture and urban planning. All this makes them a dynamic and congruent group of people, qualified to create and generate designs in which all the components and requirements are successfully integrated thanks to the sum of their shared knowledge, talents and ideas, ensuring the accomplishment of their objectives with success and professionalism.

THIS BOOK'S STRUCTURE

InnovatiON-Architecture compiles and showcases ON-A's work, focusing on their constant search for innovation in various domains and areas of application of their designs. Thus, the book has been organized as a compendium of ideas, concepts, projects, buildings and details which, based on their continuing improvement and invention, outline the criteria and foundations that are shared by all the firm's work.

In my first meetings with Eduardo Gutiérrez and Jordi Fernández in 2019, we grouped together a series of their built work and designs according to the range and the space of innovation

Meeting between Jordi Fernández, Eduardo Gutiérrez, Natalia Cabello and Ricardo Devesa starting the process of the publication structure and aims.

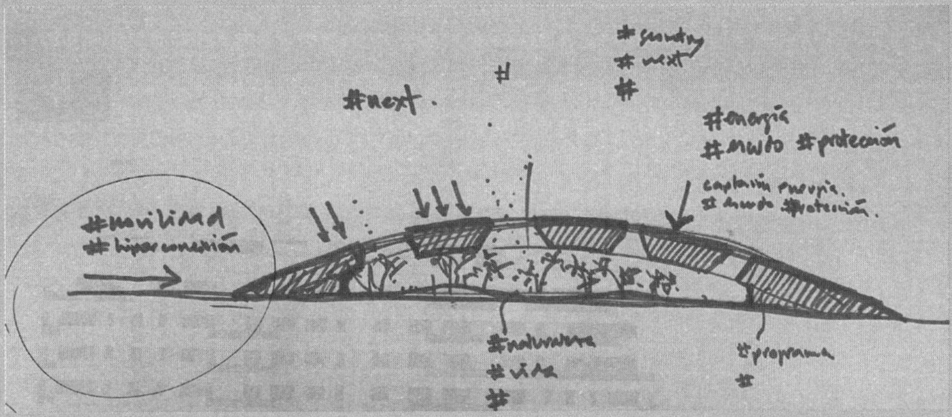

Hand drawing by ON-A about the Neon City concept.

that characterized them. In 2020, we prepared and recorded the interviews that are transcribed and included in this volume, which delve into the four main values that orient their practice (sustainability, design, emotion and technology), with the goal of understanding the different degrees of experimentation they deal with and pursue in their projects.

Each part of the book begins with a conversation, which introduces those concepts and their applications to specific projects, according to our initial groupings. Following each conversation are the detailed explanations of the architectural and urban planning projects that best illustrate the innovation parameters discussed in the transcription.

Because ON-A defines itself as a laboratory rather than a professional architecture firm, the second conversation explores their practice of architecture based on the bioclimatic and sustainable experiments and tests they have carried out from the group's inception up until the present. In that same chapter, they talk about how to incorporate the benefits of "green" by using bioarchitecture –a layer of vegetation managed through technology and ecology that incorporates the values of sustainability by way of material qualities, maintenance aspects, and benefits for users– to renaturalize cities and reconnect people with the natural environment in pursuit of a more balanced ecosystem.

The first chapter focuses on design as a jumping off point for addressing geometric control (inspired by the forms of minerals, trees and other organisms) and the encoding of information (using parametric design, BIM, and other management techniques). This methodology lets them visualize and interact with the data continuum and workflows at all stages of the development of a design, with an eye to the entire life cycle of the project.

The third conversation looks at how ON-A's designs serve as a catalyst for the creation of positive emotions on the part of the inhabitants: physical-visual wellbeing and comfort that contribute to their health and the flexibility of uses for the designed spaces. Finally, technology, which rounds out the book's fourth part, explains how it is used as a key tool to enhance their designs, based on a comprehensive material and structural modeling, of structures and building services, allowing them to control any

Working sessions between ON-A and Actar.

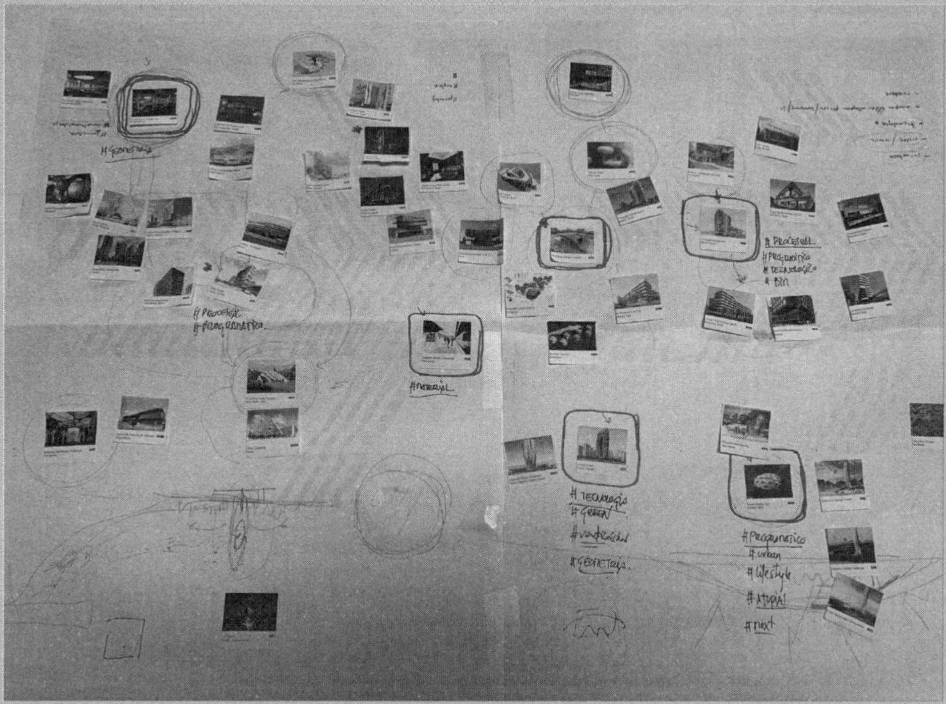

Draft of the selecction and grouping ON-A's project depending its innovations.

formal and material configuration (regardless of the elements being used: curved glass, precast GRC, wood, or other components) in the construction of their projects.

> The four parts of the book reflect the values of ON-A's practice: creating innovative, bold and emblematic buildings while committing to the paradigm shift in cities and architecture through bio-construction and the renaturalization of the environments we inhabit.

Through these four conversations, the book shows a method for innovating in architecture in different layers and in response to a powerful precept: helping to reduce the environmental impact of human intervention, improving citizens' quality of life, and promoting emotional interactions between inhabitants and their built environment.

Design_Geometry & Encoding

Note: Projects in gray are referenced in the interviews. For futher information see: https://www.on-a.es/

Sustainability_Bioclimatic & Efficiency

Emotion_Lifestyle & Inhabiting

Technology_Materials & Techniques

ON-A emulates nature's optimization of resources and geometries. Their design drivers propose continuous forms understood as a whole.

ON-A means "wave", a synthesis of nature as a complex but parameterizable form that can be controlled by codes.

Design

Geometry & Encoding

RICARDO What role does geometry play in your designs? Where does your inspiration come from? Why do you use complex geometries, and what are the reasons for their application and their advantages?

JORDI Before we founded ON-A in 2005, Eduardo and I were both fascinated by geometry and complex forms. I used my final degree project to research computer programs that develop geometries, and that's when I started with Rhinoceros. As I learned more about it, I said to myself: "I need to take advantage of this" and I started using it with Enric Ruiz-Geli. But I'd already used it for my degree project because my design had inflatable roofs and unfolding geometries, so we investigated that whole idea of "unfolding" back then. The relationship with nature, its forms, how its geometries are generated, is something else that we liked.

In fact, everything came to a head in our first project, the 5 Sentidos Lounge Bar, a foundational project where we first had the opportunity to develop our ideas and actually build them. It was intended as a place to experience the five senses, so we created a structural mesh. We wanted to create an envelope that would resolve both the interior and the exterior at the same time, while also creating the private areas requested by the client.

The geometry we developed was totally adapted to the site, modeled piece by piece, so it could be adjusted to fit the existing columns and floor structure. The way we built it was entirely through experimentation, unfolding the geometries so we would be able cut them, fold them, and install them on the site. And it was all possible thanks to a metalworker, Ramon Presta, a dedicated craftsman with a real passion for his work. He let us work side by side with him to develop the first prototypes, doing tests and trials in his workshop; that way we could put together an exact budget for the client and make sure the pieces would work. First, we made a prototype of a node, because the model was infinitesimal, and we wanted to see what would happen when we gave it a thickness. Then we made a model of one of the private areas on a 1:10 scale. Then we laser cut all the pieces. In short, all the ingredients for an initial foundational work came together, and from there we decided what ON-A was going to be.

RICARDO In the bar project, for example, the vector mesh defines the structure and the space at the same time. That's something you've used later in other projects, in the structure of a skyscraper, which ends up defining the building geometrically. How do you make that scalar leap with complex geometries?

EDUARDO Rather than complex geometries, we like optimized geometries. We try to emulate the perfect optimization that we see in nature.

The bar is a good example of how a single element can be used as structure and as a spatial divider at the same time. It's the same process when we want to translate that into a different kind of building, like a skyscraper where the structure is shown on the façade. What's the best way to generate a structure which in turn performs multiple functions? Nature knows how to do that and has been doing it forever. It isn't a "naive" complexity, making something complex just because you feel like it. It meets certain criteria within the natural laws of physics. Obviously, there is always an aesthetic aspect, because that geometric formalization can happen in many different ways, but there is an idea of optimizing processes.

When we were designing the bar, we looked at the structure of bones, a single material that creates spaces and cavities. With geometry and a material, you get a bone cell.

RICARDO As architects trained in Barcelona, have you been influenced by Gaudí's work? For him, all the elements in nature are articulated and connected. The continuity between elements is a result of optimization, but interestingly enough it is also beautiful. To what extent did his work influence you?

JORDI Despite the fact that Gaudí isn't discussed at all at the Barcelona School of Architecture – it seems like he never even existed – the influence of his work is clearly present. In fact, we feel like Gaudí, today, would be Zaha Hadid. He would design parametric architecture, complex forms; he would analyze nature and look at how to generate those geometries using a computer. Our bar design is a bit Gaudinian in that sense, inspired by nature; it's a continuous form that is understood as a whole.

EDUARDO Gaudí was limited by the technology of his time. That's where the big leap forward comes from. Today, we can technify the whole process and come up with much more precise and much more optimized solutions. Aesthetically, the result may be completely different, even if we're drawing from the same source – which is nature. Before, everything had to be built with bricks and mosaic; now we can print structures with millimetric precision. Gaudí used to hang sandbags to study the natural loads. Then he'd flip that structure, and it would give him the arches and the vaults. Now, we can figure it all out very precisely using computers.

JORDI In Gaudí's time, his work was possible because there were industrialists and craftsmen who had the skills to build it. Today, those trades have been lost, but they've been replaced with technology: we have 3D printers and CNC machines that can generate any form using any material. So, the technological leap is a factor.

EDUARDO In architecture, rationalist designs use straight abstract lines, which aren't natural.

We go a little more to the root. We end up with those optimizations, or those abstractions, but we begin from the foundation of the natural reality of things and how the forces of nature behave, and that results in a complex geometry. We see it as complex in terms of our visual tradition of architecture. But technology offers other models, like Star Wars, or science fiction movies where buildings almost shape themselves; they're living entities, they don't have a defined rectangular form. Now, we can meld with the reality of nature.

JORDI Our interest in geometry is based on controlling it, regardless of whether it's simple or complex.

We treat each project as different. If a complex project comes along, we have to be able to build it. If it's meant to be simple, like the house with the green roof, or the Drassanes Metro Station, it has to be functional. Geometries and natural shapes are in our collective imagination. At the office, we have a lot of books on natural forms. Even our name ON-A, aside from "On Architects" – as in, active architects – also means 'wave' [*ona*], which is the synthesis of nature: a simple form that gives rise, in the aggregate, to a very complex, and parameterizable, form. A wave is a mathematical function, so it can be controlled and simulated virtually.

At ON-A, we have that relationship between geometry, complexity and control.

RICARDO Can you tell me how you applied these principles for the Drassanes Metro Station project?

EDUARDO A metro station is a transportation-related non-place, where there are constant flows. In terms of functionality, the flows have to work perfectly. That's why the design has those

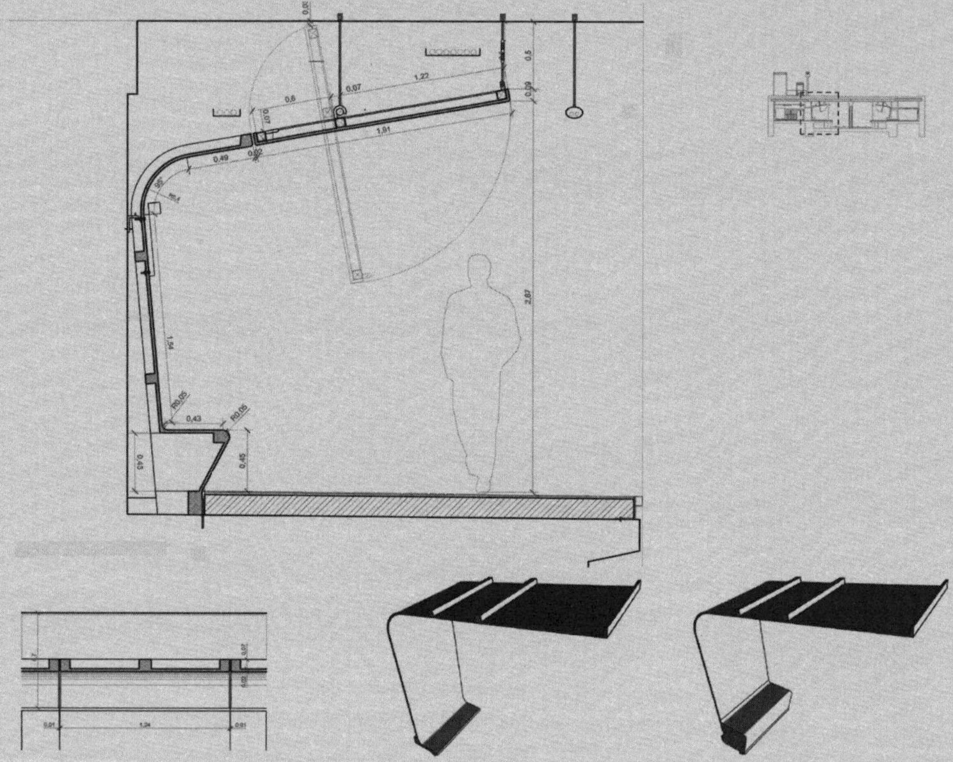

Section of Drassanes metro station, Barcelona.

curves and the fluidity that supports the use of the station. Yet the lighting in the project is entirely different. It has intersections and densities where more light is needed: for example, at the ticket machines. So, the lumens are optimized in that space, instead of installing two parallel strips of lighting across the entire station equally. This layout, which may seem complex and chaotic, is optimized for the function it needs to fulfill at the time. The envelope is white and continuous, without edges, because it directs the flow of people and is easier to clean. It's the synthesis of something that is very simple and complex at the same time.

JORDI The lights in the station also have a poetic component, to symbolize the intersections between people's lives that take place in a station. There's the component of emotion that we always talk about, along with innovation and technology.

Connecting corridor and platform of Drassanes metro station, Barcelona.

The lights in the station also have a poetic component, to symbolize the intersections between people's lives that take place in a station. There's the component of emotion that we always talk about, along with innovation and technology.

The uniformity of the interior cladding is designed as a reflective extension of the station's artificial lighting. This creates an overall effect of brightness, nuanced by the breadth of the surfaces that extend upward as a continuation of the pavement.

RICARDO I'd like to hear about another concept that's also very important to you: encoding. You waim for a systematization of processes with the elements you use, so that they are protocolized and can be repeated. Plus, with encoding there is a desire for exhaustive control of what you're building and executing.

EDUARDO **Since we're aware that there are physical limitations when it comes to controlling a large amount of information, we need to have a system, an encoding of the process. Using technologies like BIM, not only can we define the geometries, but we can associate them with data that lets us encode everything. Our design process can be much riskier and yet efficient at the same time.**

Riskier in the sense that we can arrive at complex geometries, but at the same time we have them much more under control. It's like DNA, the code that defines each part of a person. The process of encoding in architecture is the same. Each element has its own code and its relationship with the other elements around it.

The ON-A projects where those codes are most important include, obviously, the Lounge Bar, where each piece was different in terms of type and in how it related to the next piece (or multiple others, because it could be a five-part node), which then determined the necessary inclination and the intersections between the different planes. Another example is the Cricursa stand, where each edge and each pane of glass had its own encoding, which made it possible to assemble and disassemble the same stand for different trade fairs.

JORDI Encoding is essential when you're dealing with special (or complex) architectures. On the other hand, if you're building a brick façade, you just need to stack one brick on top of the other. But if you're developing a unique project with unique pieces and each one is different, encoding is absolutely essential.

Modeling of Stand Cricursa, Barcelona.

Another example is the roof structure for the Seminary of Tarragona, where the layout of the openings and elements corresponded to what was underneath. In other words, the beams are directed toward specific points that could support the weight of the entire roof. If we had just been designing a grid, we wouldn't have needed to code it; you can repeat the same elements and that's it. But, in this case, there were also two codes: the structural code and the lighting code. That combination resulted in an added directional component, which made each circle or opening different. To generate that, we had to encode each of the circles – with a specific radius, a specific form – and each of the beams. Encoding was absolutely necessary in building them. The interesting thing is that, today, technology lets us maintain efficiency and control costs using industrial machining processes, numerical control, to generate a series of different, unique parts.

Each edge and each pane of glass had its own encoding, which made it possible to assemble and disassemble the same stand for different trade fairs.

Cricursa Stand: The geometry is inspired by the crystalline forms of silica, the base component of glass. Its properties are transferred onto the stand, making it into a large-scale digital geode.

...Although it is a conventional and marketable building, we built the façade using unique elements to create a more fluid appearance for the envelope.

The Rengle Tower, Mataró. Its façade uses industrialized elements, giving prominence to curved GRC panels with different geometries, allowing for building quickly and economically.

We are also big believers in industrialization and bringing architecture closer to the world of the automotive industry or aeronautics and being able to finish pieces in the workshop in a controlled way before they're installed on site.

RICARDO The architecture of modernity was based on a Euclidean, Cartesian geometry regulated by proportions, whereas an optimized geometry – like what we see in nature – behaves more like a relational element. That's also why the development of digital technologies has made it possible for us to build these buildings. How do you apply encoding to the construction of large housing blocks or even entire cities?

JORDI For example, in the Rengle Tower in Mataró, a large post-crisis residential project, although it is a conventional and marketable building, we built the façade using unique elements to create a more fluid appearance for the envelope. It also required encoding, but on a different level, since there were different molds, which resulted from a process of optimization.

Using the minimum number of molds and gestures, we obtained the maximum number of combinations to give the façade its richness.

It's one of those things that isn't noticeable at first glance, but everyone who passes the building remembers it. Those small gestures help you avoid uniformity in the openings. All this is scalable, of course, and we've applied it in other projects, like the Smart Mesh Building in Taiwan from 2012, where we used a reactive smart mesh. We determined a series of points, which were chosen randomly to add that variety. We started with the minimum opening for a residential building – in terms of light, views, etc. – and then we generated a gradient up to the maximum opening.

Smart Mesh Building: It is a building with a volume made from three arms that twist around a central Z axis.
Smart Mesh Building. --See pag. 44--

EDUARDO We use geometric complexity in two ways. In the Taiwan building, the complexity comes from the optimization of a structural geometry. In Mataró, on the other hand, the complexity is emotional. The building could be built just the same without it, but it adds something emotionally: there's something extra. And we achieved that through a minimal gesture, which is concise and controlled, both in terms of process and in terms of cost, but which also has a function: as a façade where an enclosure is needed, as a railing, and as sun protection. Everything has its reason for being. And it was produced using a single curved mold, everything in elevation and in plan. The straight extrusions also began with a mold that we modified depending on the necessary width. In other words, the entire building was resolved using three molds. That's part of the optimization that is made possible by encoding.

RICARDO How do you apply those principles when you're building an urban environment, a master plan, like in the Neom city project?

EDUARDO In the same way. Traditionally, cities are organized into large avenues with buildings along the edges, but we asked ourselves whether that was the best way, or whether that's been the convention for the past 300 years because that's what was possible. Now, things are different. We can develop a master plan that is also a building in itself, which is also a shelter, and controls the city's climate, while capturing energy, etc. The possibilities are endless. So, we started looking at what kind of geometric structures can encompass all of that. And we started with a spherical dome, because that gave us both solar protection and solar capture, it offered a structural solution to avoid large spans, and it had the potential to generate interior microclimates. You start stringing together ideas and making connections, and you see how the geometry starts getting more complex, because the same geometry offers a solution for more and more aspects, and it starts to make sense. It's like the intertwining of human DNA we were talking about earlier, but in architecture.

RICARDO Your geometric innovation isn't just a formal innovation, which would be vacant; rather, everything has its reason for being. And that implies beauty and, therefore, emotion, which is your mantra. What is your idea of beauty?

EDUARDO **Our idea of beauty is genetic or procedural.** Ultimately, human beings are changeable; the essence is the same and every moment has its beauty, because every moment is a different function. That's what it amounts to. Or natural beauty, because plants have a type of genetics that supports their way of being, and at the same time they're beautiful and they elicit emotion.

JORDI I would say it's an evolutionary beauty. In nature, evolution makes perfection – that is, there is a function which, through evolution, becomes defined in an optimized geometry. The paradigmatic example would be a honeycomb. It's pure mathematics. It's an evolutionary and interactive geometry. I mentioned the Seminary of Tarragona before, which had several layers: structure, light, and emotion. That generated a geometry which was specific to that site. For Neom, we had a tabula rasa, a flat space. That's why we came up with a semi-sphere, which is the best dome, and it worked in terms of structure. Then we introduced the hexagons, identical openings, arranged rationally. Then we analyzed the sun exposure and distributed the solar panels in the areas where the software indicated there was the most sun exposure. In the end, there are a lot of layers that contribute to making it possible for the geometry, the forms, the openings to be reactive. Technology today lets us do that. That's why we talk about reactive, interactive and, therefore, also evolutionary geometry.

EDUARDO Another example is our skyscraper in Riyadh, Saudi Arabia: The Blade, from 2015. We took advantage of the convection generated by skyscrapers to make the building skin open like gills to capture the movement of air and generate

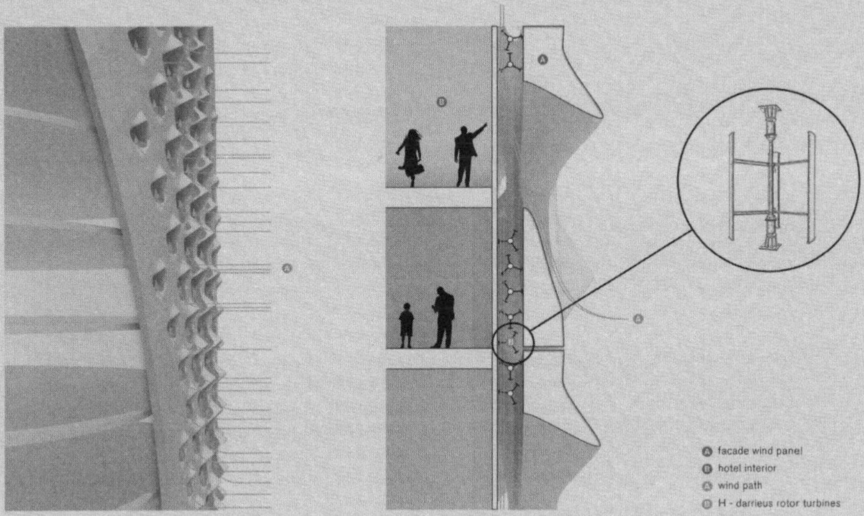

The Blade Tower, aerodynamic skyscraper: Wind turbines detail. Each panel incorporates turbines, and the diameter of the openings varies geometrically in order to promote natural ventilation in parallel with the cooling system that takes advantage of rainwater harvesting.
--See page 74--

energy within the skyscraper itself. First, we perforated the building to avoid the wind screen effect, so that the air could move through at three points which we "greenified". At the same time, we took advantage of the air currents that develop around high-rise buildings to generate energy. The gills that appear on the side of the building are complex, but they all have a function: here, it was to capture energy within the building. In turn, that generates a form, which is beautiful, but it is not intentional for its own sake.

RICARDO In the architecture of modernity, form is the result of resolving a function, understood in a very basic way, without any interaction, adaptation, proactivity or reactivity with respect to the phenomena around it that justify it. In your architecture, geometry is more than a schematic functional determinism; it's much more interactive with everything that's going on: including energetic and climatological aspects, or material and economic optimization, for example.

EDUARDO Geometry has Big Data and other associated functions. It isn't geometry for geometry's sake. Geometry has data, whether it has to do with material optimization, energy capture, or whatever requirements you have at the time. How all those parameters are controlled is determined by the encoding. When all the elements are different and have particular functions, you need encoding.

JORDI In the project for the National Water Company of Saudi Arabia, commissioned by the water company in Riyadh, water is represented on the façade in river-like forms. The building begins with a square floor plan on the ground floor and a larger twisting floor above it. This generates an optimized office building, where the floors expand as they get higher. The highest floors are the most valuable, where you have more surface area. Normally it's the other way around, the highest floors are the smallest. That gives us a simple geometry in terms of the floor plan, which is functional. But then we add these gestures on the façade that are related to the program and the company's values. Depending on which elevation you look at, it looks straight up and down, or it has an ascending form. We also incorporated this relationship with water visually, using blue lights at night that simulate the flow of water. In the end, there's this idea of bringing layers together: program, functionality, geometry, the client's needs, what you want to convey.

RICARDO Who are your contemporary references with regard to the optimized and relational use of geometry? Whom do you identify with, and who else do you think works along similar lines?

JORDI In general, we have our eye on a lot of architects, a lot of interesting projects. Obviously, Zaha Hadid is a real reference for forms in the sense of those fluid geometries. She was totally groundbreaking and innovative in that regard, and she created a clear imagery in contemporary architecture. We're also interested in Norman Foster with his processes, innovation and management. Each of our projects has its own language, which comes from many different components, as we were saying.

EDUARDO In addition to work by other architects, we also draw on literary references. I remember that when I was doing my final degree project, the theoretical foundation was based on Roger Penrose, this idea of the scales of the universe, the patterns that are generated from macrostructures, like the universe, and how they are related to atomic microstructures. There are those laws, those processes that are physically very distant, but they're present in essence. When you study architecture, they teach you that a portico runs in a straight line and has spans of five meters. But you can optimize that in a different way if you apply more fundamental concepts based on nature. We've also been influenced by Paul Virilio, Giles Deleuze, etc. Also, everything that was being published at the time in magazines like *Quaderns d'arquitectura i urbanisme, Verb,* etc.

National Water Company Tower, complex geometries shapes: Overall volume of the tower is twisted to define a wave-like profile. **--See pag. 52--**

SMART MESH BUILDING
TAIPEI

Located in the center of Taipei, the most populous city in the PRC, this new apartment building is almost 100 m high.

The triangular shape of the plot allowed for experimenting with new forms of parametric architecture. The result of this adaptive play is a building with a volume made from three arms that twist around a central Z axis. The true singularity of the building is its façade, composed of a double skin formed from rhomboid elements that are adapted, with different-sized openings, depending on the orientation and sun exposure. This parametric structure also offers views over the city of Taipei.

During the design process, integrated optimized parameters were used to generate an energy-efficient tower. Working with this advanced digital techiques, allows to develop an original, organic and exclusive product. In addition, thanks to its shapes, at night the building shines like a geometric lantern in the middle of the city.

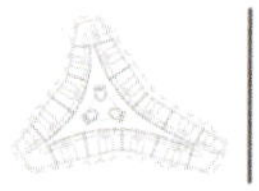

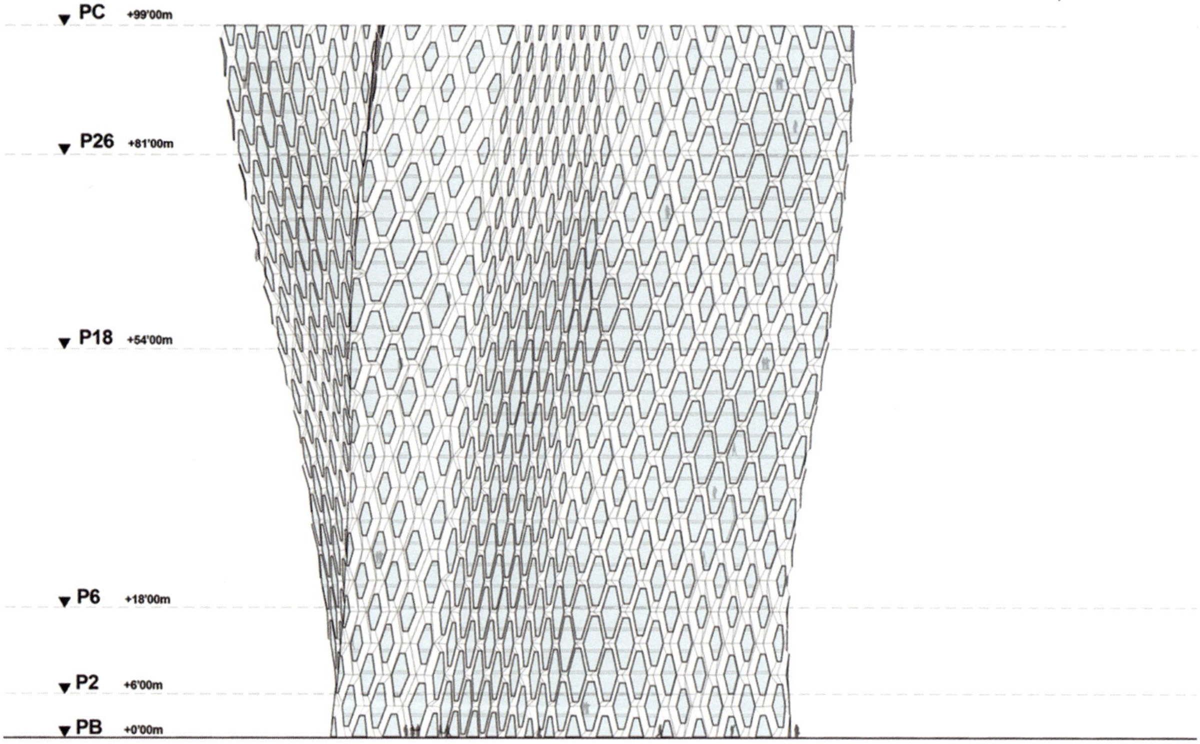

The triangular shape of the plot allowed for experimenting with new forms of parametric architecture. The result of this adaptive play is a building with a volume made from three arms that twist around a central Z axis.

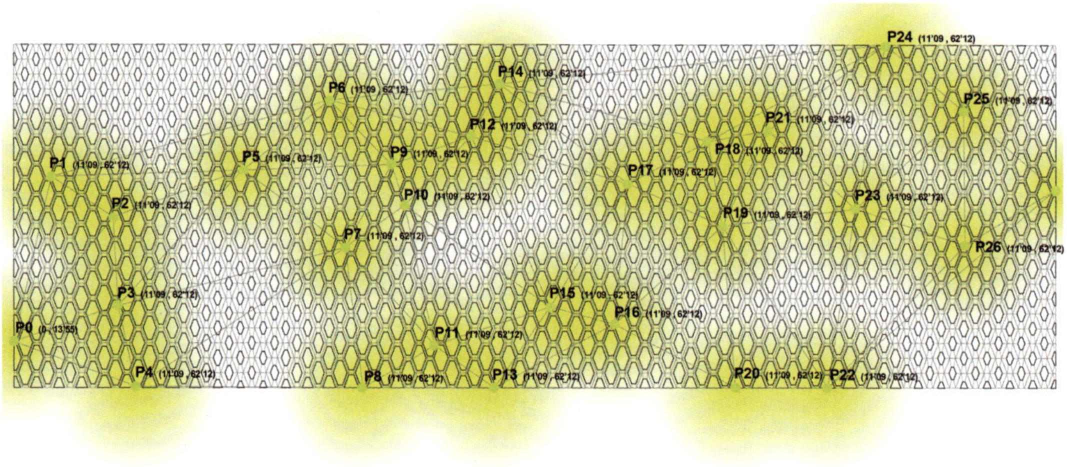

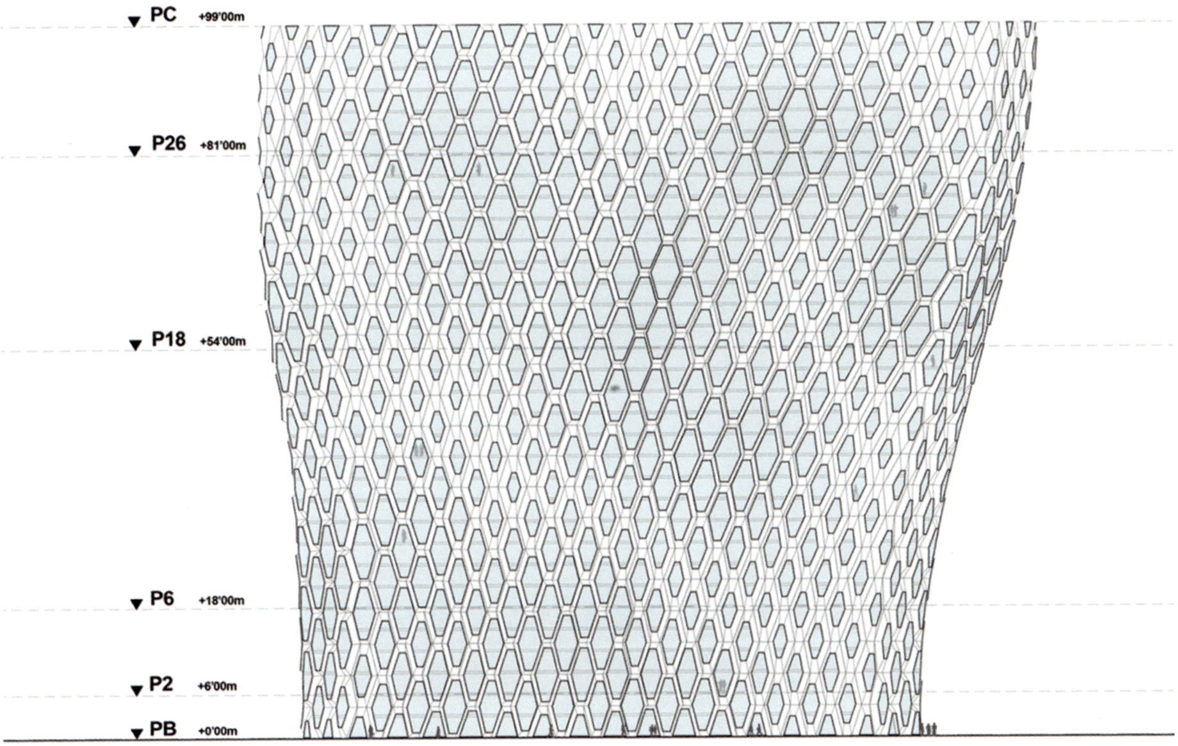

Organic
Parametric
Versatile
Efficient

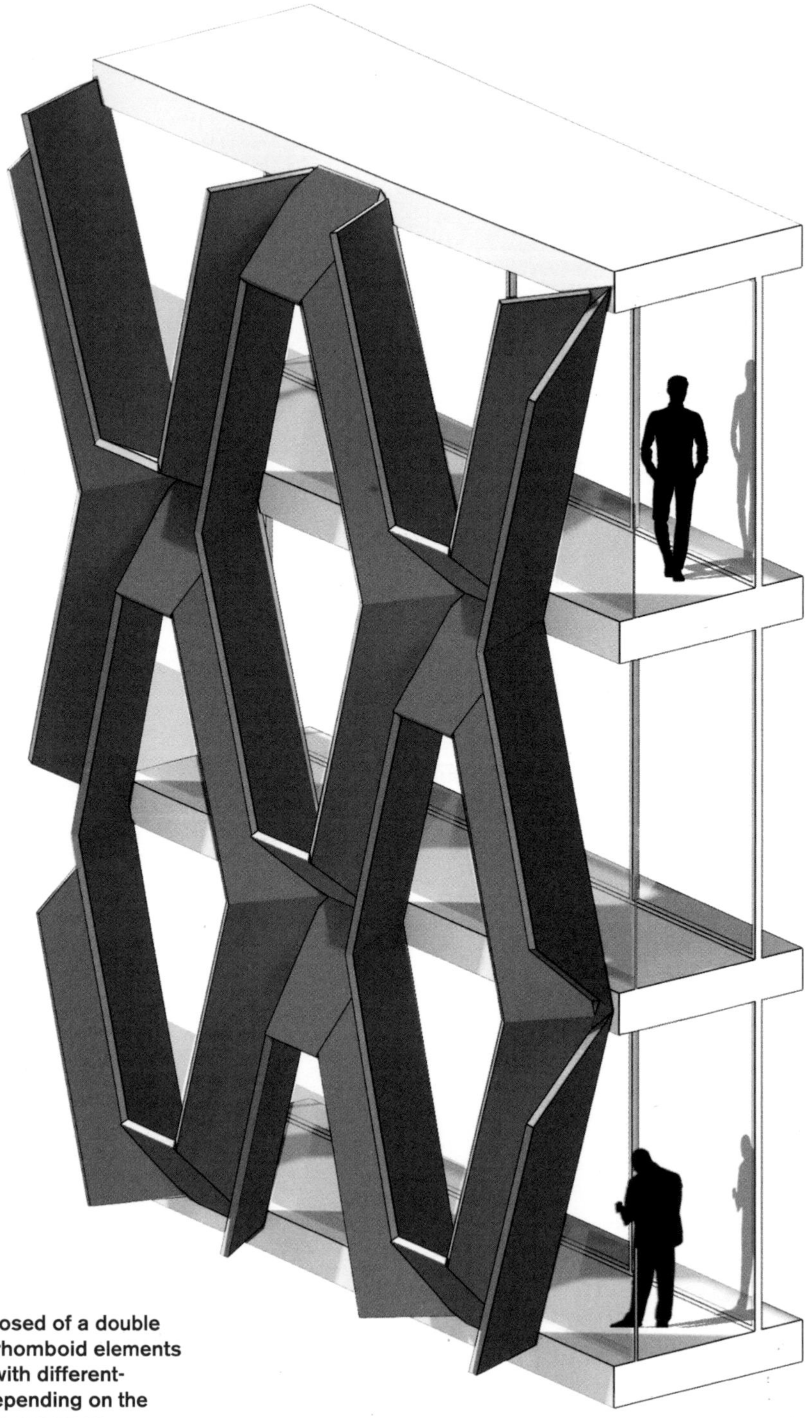

Its façade is composed of a double skin formed from rhomboid elements that are adapted, with different-sized openings, depending on the orientation and sun exposure.

NATIONAL WATER COMPANY TOWER
RIYADH

The tower intended to house the offices of the National Water Company is located on one of the main thoroughfares in the city of Riyadh.

With a height of 160 m, the program is structured on the ground floor with a lobby followed by three mezzanine floors, 20 floors of offices with coworking areas and meeting rooms, and the final two floors for the exclusive use of company executives. The overall volume of the tower is twisted to define a wave-like profile.

The façade flows along the same lines, making reference to the forms of moving water, further defining its appearance at night using artificial lighting installed along the structural profiles.

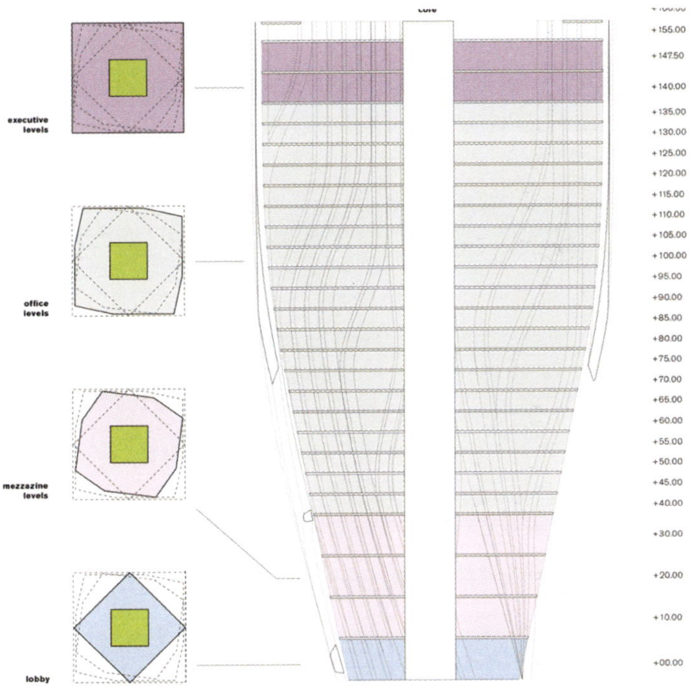

section A-A

south - east elevation

Twisted Parametric Complexity

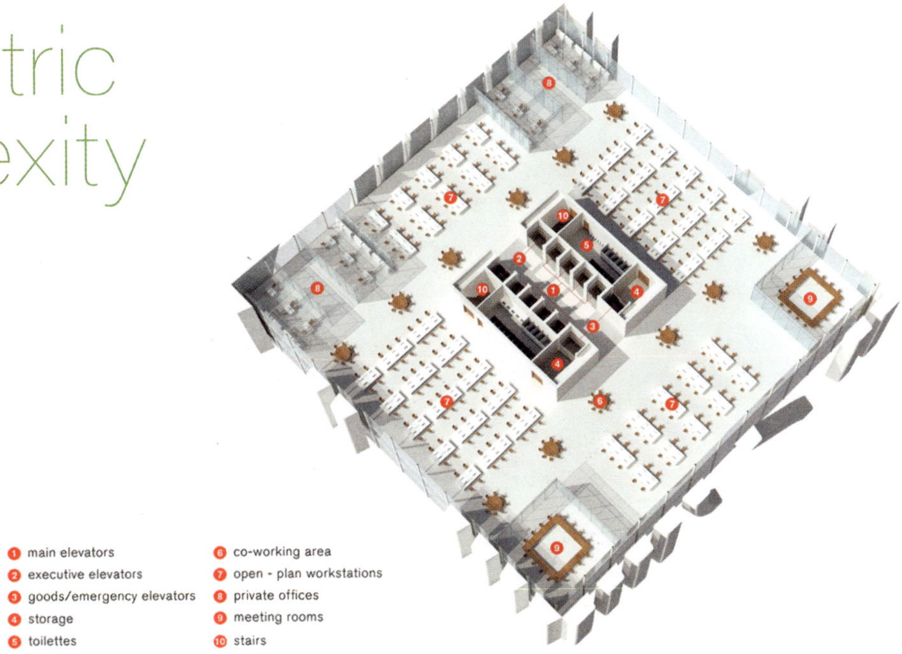

south elevation

east elevation

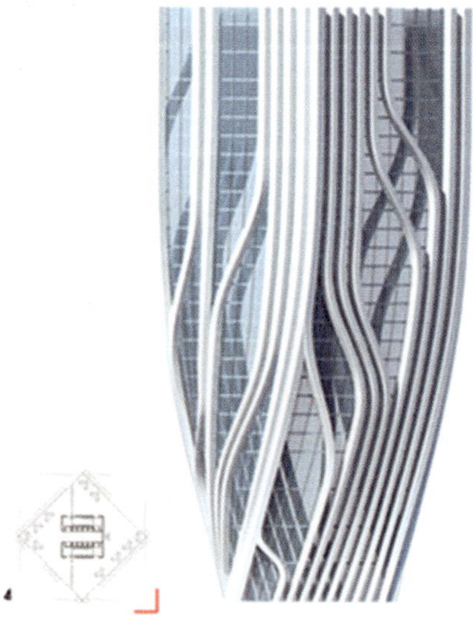

south - east elevation

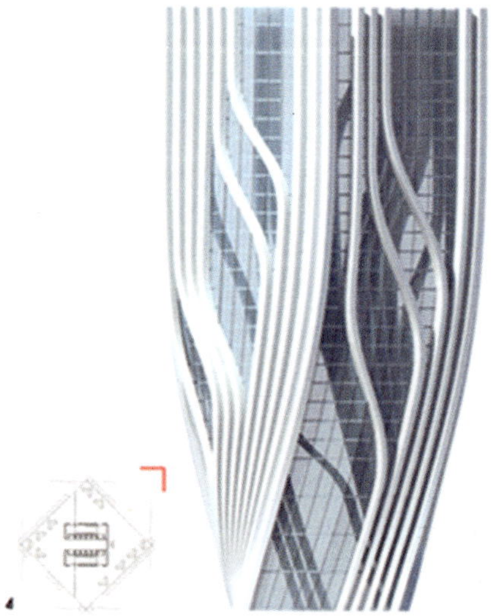

north - east elevation

Using complex geometric shapes and turn them into parameterized elements in the model, we obtain unique designs.

north elevation

west elevation

waves / water reference

north - west elevation

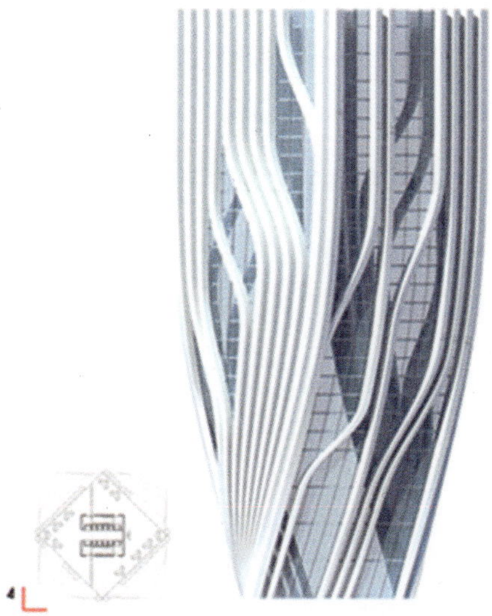

south - west elevation

BLIDA CENTER TOWER

BLIDA

A new multipurpose tower was designed for an area undergoing an urban transformation near the city of Algiers. The program combines different functions such as a healthcare and social services center, commercial premises, and a residential area for a total of 25,000 m^2.

At the base of the tower is a large shopping center with restaurants, and the healthcare center is located on the middle floors. The remaining floors are allocated for residential use.

The project is located near the university and is well connected to public transportation, such as trains. The volumes are hinged together and extend with broad cantilevers and terraces in different directions, forming a large park that promotes cleaner air and helps improve residents' access to green areas. The façade, made up of horizontal strips of white GRC (glass reinforced concrete), generates small overhangs to offer protection from the sun. The interior façade, on the other hand, varies according to the program it houses, generating a series of architectural solutions that all adhere to a similar concept.

Medical center
Bida center

Medical center
Blida center

Versatile Efficient

residential
hospital
shopping centre

1 shopping centre entrance
2 shopping centre
3 restaurant
4 terrace

5 hospital rooms
6 nursing
7 hospital reception
8 medical consultations
9 waiting room
10 terrace

11 elevators
12 housing
13 housing terrace

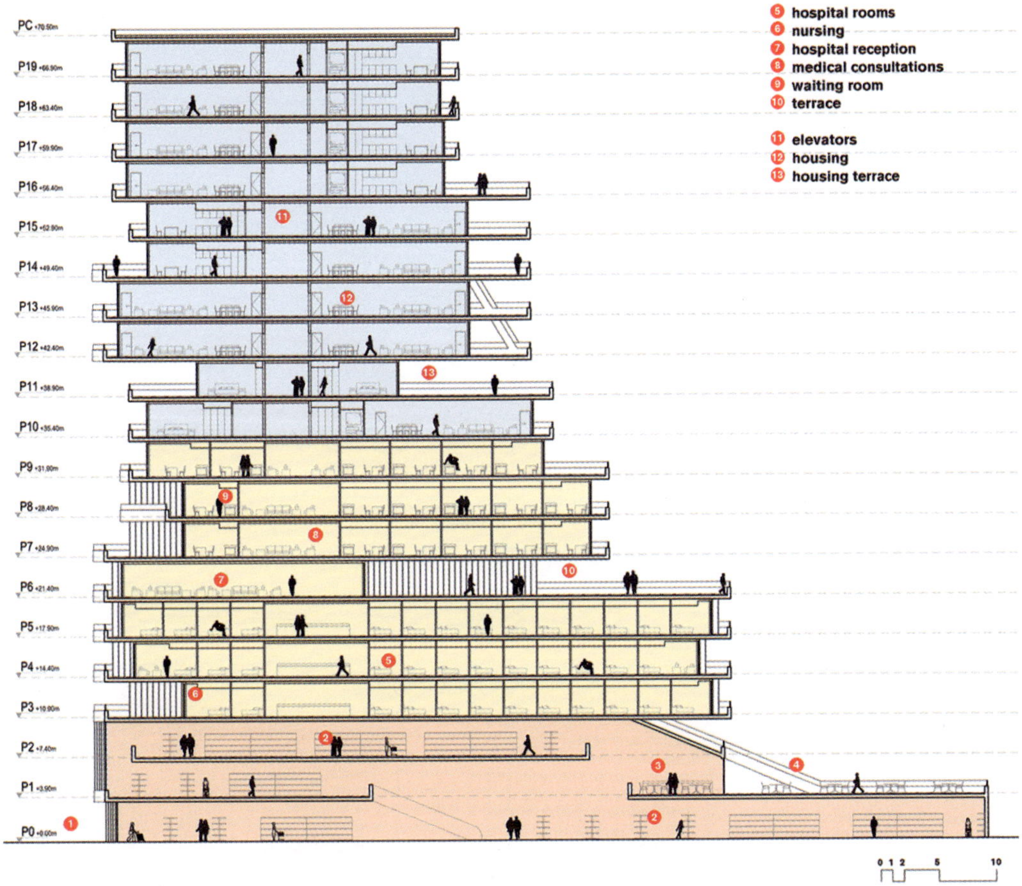

shopping centre	5.150,00 m2
P0	3.150,00 m2
P1	925,00 m2
P2	1.075,00 m2

hospital	10.289,00 m2
P3	2.086,00 m2
P4	1.461,00 m2
P5	1.570,00 m2
P6	1.653,00 m2
P7	1.101,00 m2
P8	1.209,00 m2
P9	1.209,00 m2

residential	9.558,00 m2
P10	1.202,00 m2
P11	780,00 m2
P12	935,00 m2
P13	935,00 m2
P14	856,00 m2
P15	856,00 m2
P16	998,50 m2
P17	998,50 m2
P18	998,50 m2
P19	998,50 m2

TOTAL 24.997,00 m2

PROGRAMME OF USES
BTP multi-use building | Blida

5 SENTIDOS LOUNGE BAR
GIRONA, SPAIN

The Lounge & Bar is located in a summer resort town on the Costa Brava. The resources used in the design are intended to stimulate all the senses: there are visual, chromatic and auditory effects which contribute to the user's overall experience, surrounded by an organic and particularly complex geometry. The uniqueness of this project stems from its structure, which may seem somewhat confusing at first but gradually becomes perceptible and ordered: a branching system that hierarchizes each space, while generating a transparency that results in a continuity which allows for interaction between users.

Taking a regular footprint with a floor area of 200 m^2, a long bar is surrounded by the two areas reserved for groups, and the common spaces that foster more interaction nearer to the bathrooms. The language of the structural matrix appears in plan through a pattern on the flooring that adapts to the geometry of the bar and the VIP zone. The general design concept is based on generating a three-dimensional steel mesh which, in addition to forming the volume of the entrance, is pulled into the interior of the existing building as an extension that can be adapted to meet the programmatic requirements using the same material conditions. The spaces are framed by the openings formed by a three-dimensional mesh made up of more than 1,500 faces, offering complexity and richness to the overall appearance of the project. The layout appears to shift and change according to the lighting conditions and visitors' vantage points.

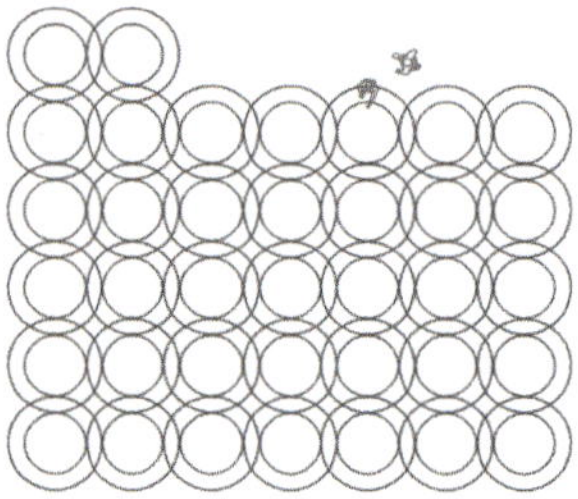

37 table units
148 people

Uniqueness
Structural Matrix
Geometry

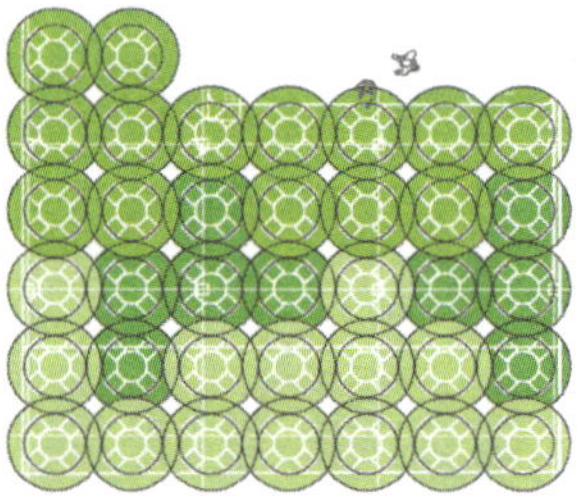

zone A: 14 units (37,83%)
zone B: 14 units (37,83%)
zone C: 9 units (24,32%)

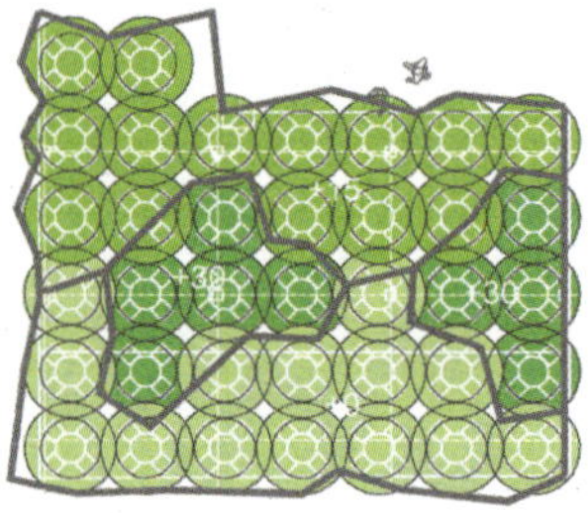

zone A: 67.10 m²
zone B: 72.27 m²
zone C: 51.12 m²

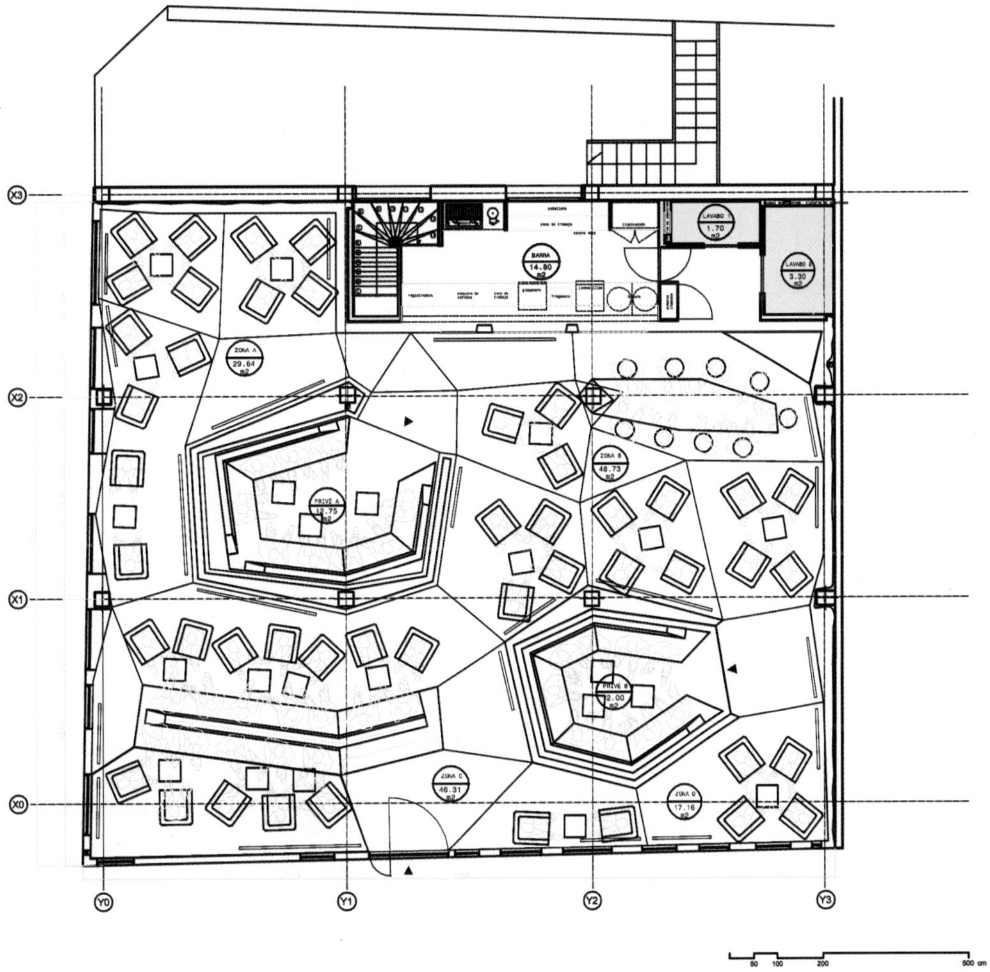

Taking a regular footprint with a floor area of 200 m², a long bar is surrounded by the two areas reserved for groups, and the common spaces that foster more interaction nearer to the bathrooms.

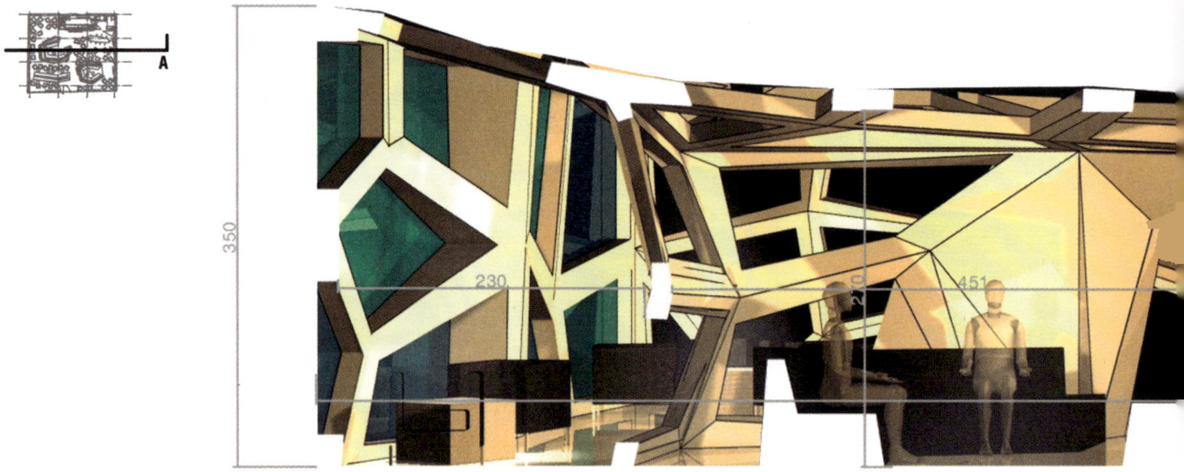

The spaces are framed by the openings formed by the structural matrix: a three-dimensional mesh made up of more than 1,500 faces, offering complexity and richness to the overall appearance of the project.

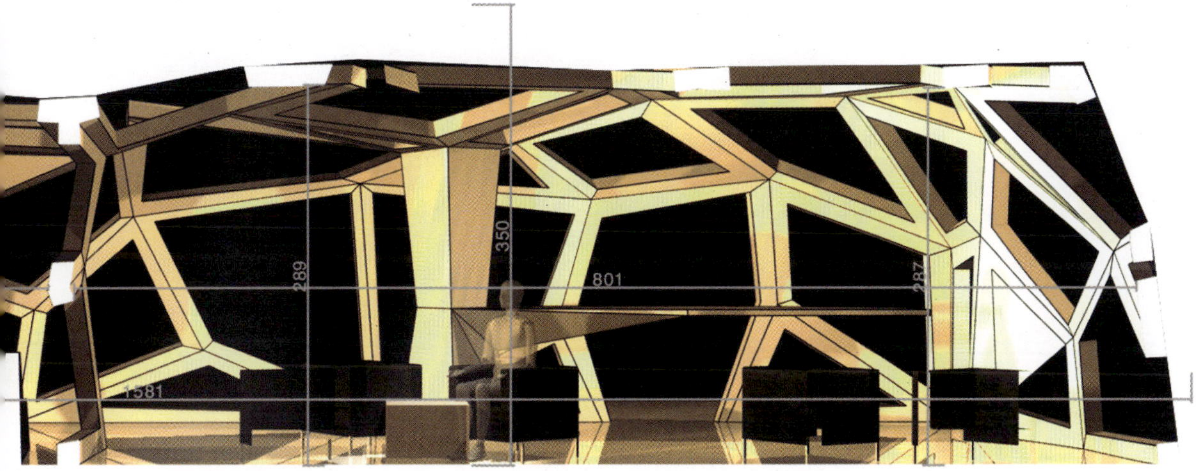
350
289
801
287
1581

1587
326
641

Lighting was a fundamental parameter in generating the atmosphere for the main rooms.

The transition from day to night is reflected in an overlapping of night scenes and atmospheres using RGB fluorescence to create chromatic combinations that transform the project into a generator of visual impressions.

THE BLADE TOWER
RIYADH

This large 610-meter-high hotel complex, located in a strategic area of Riyadh, close to the business district and the city center, is a skyscraper that includes spa services, a sky bar-restaurant and conference center. Its program also incorporates three garden floors at strategic points of the building that function aerodynamically as windbreaks.

As part of the conceptual design, renewable energy mechanisms are incorporated into the façade and the building, following a modular system of parametrically designed panels. Each panel incorporates turbines, and the diameter of the openings varies geometrically in order to promote natural ventilation in parallel with the cooling system that takes advantage of rainwater harvesting.

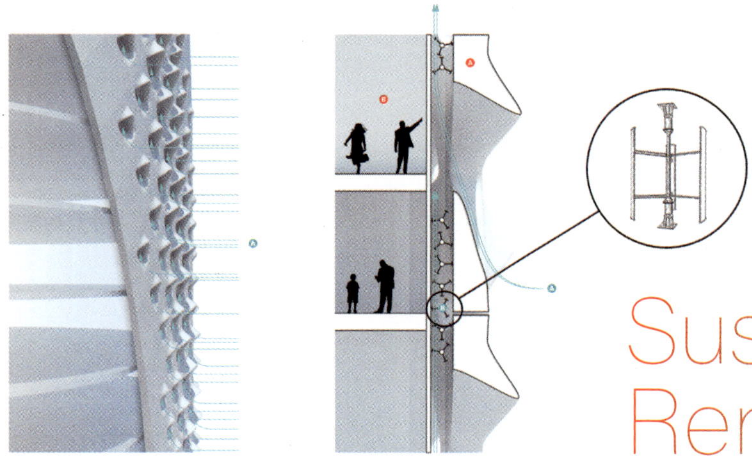

- Ⓐ facade wind panel
- Ⓑ hotel interior
- Ⓐ wind path
- Ⓑ H - darrieus rotor turbines

Sustainability Renewable Energies Aerodynamism

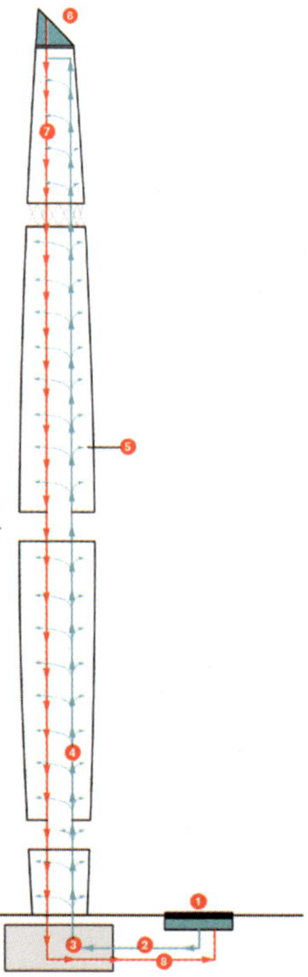

water management and cooling system

1. underground rain water collector
2. water cooling in the cold ground
3. pumping station
4. water travelling up
5. natural colling of floor plates and slabs
6. rain water colection
7. warm water travelling back into the ground
8. water being pumped back into the collector

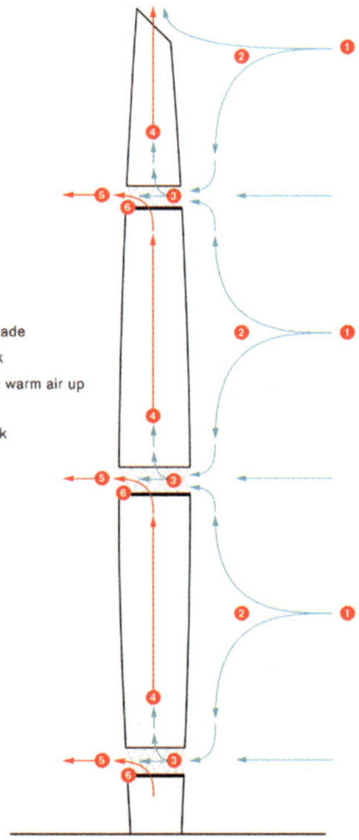

aerodynamics and natural ventilation

1. wind approaching the building
2. wind breaking when in collision with the facade
3. wind being pressured trough the wind break
4. cooller air entering the atriums and pushing warm air up
5. warm air exiting
6. reinforced floor slabs under each wind break

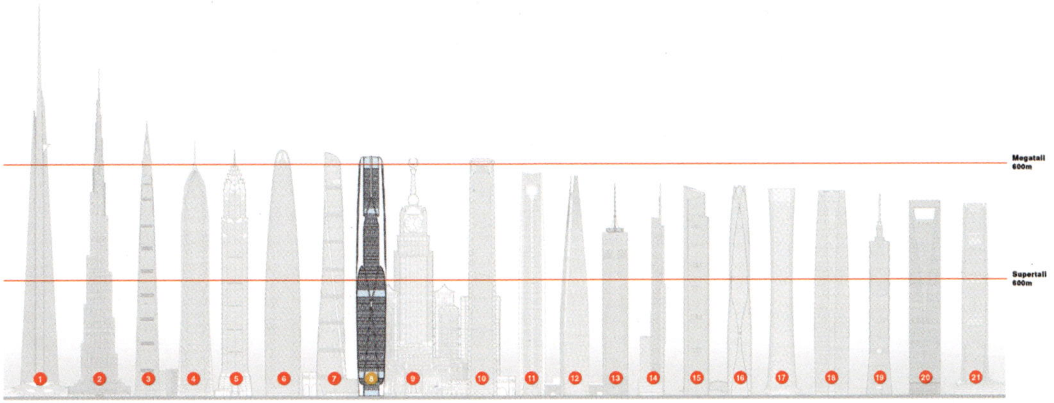

1. Kingdom Tower (Jeddah, Saudi Arabia) / 1000m / 2019
2. Burj Khalifa (Dubai, United Arab Emirates) / 828m / 2010
3. Suzhou Zhongnan Center (Suzhou, China) / 729m / 2020
4. Ping An Finance Center (Shenzen, China) / 660m / 2016
5. Signature Tower (Jakarta, Indonesia) / 638m / 2020
6. Wuhan Greenland Center (Wuhan, China) / 636m / 2017
7. Shanghai Tower (Shanghai, China) / 632m / 2015
8. The Blade Tower (Riyadh, Saudi Arabia) / 610m
9. Makkah Royal Clock (Mecca, Saudi Arabia) / 601m / 2012
10. Goldin Finance 117 (Tianjin, China) / 597m / 2016
11. Pearl of the North (Shenyang, China) / 565m / 2018
12. Lotte World Tower (Seoul, South Korea) / 555m / 2016
13. One World Trade Center (New York City, USA) / 541m / 2014
14. Nordstrom Tower (New York City, USA) / 541m / 2018
15. CTF Finance Centre (Guangzhou, China) / 530m / 2016
16. Tianjin Chow Tai Fook Binghai Center (Tianjin, China) / 530m / 2018
17. Zhongguo Zun (Beijing, China) / 528m / 2018
18. Dalian Greenland Center (Dalian, China) / 518m / 2018
19. Taipei 101 (Taipei, Taiwan) / 508m / 2004
20. Shanghai World Financial Center (Shanghai, China) / 492m / 2008
21. International Commerce Centre (Hong Kong, China) / 484m / 2010

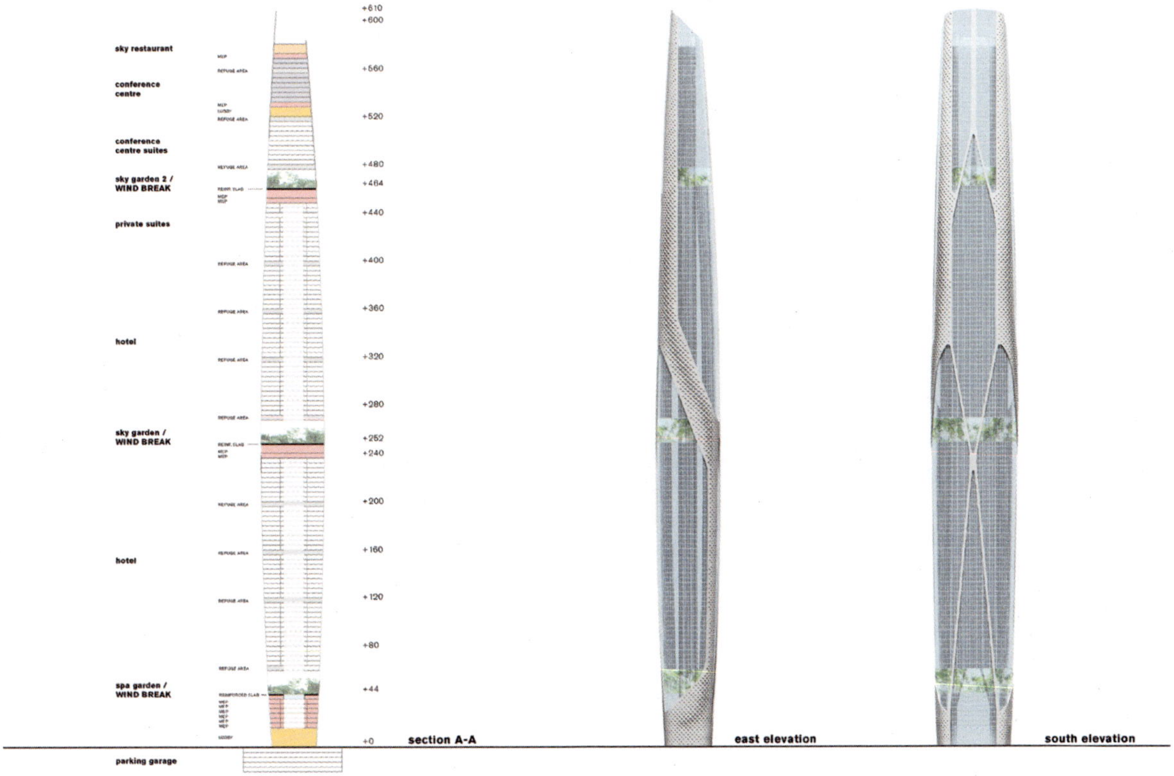

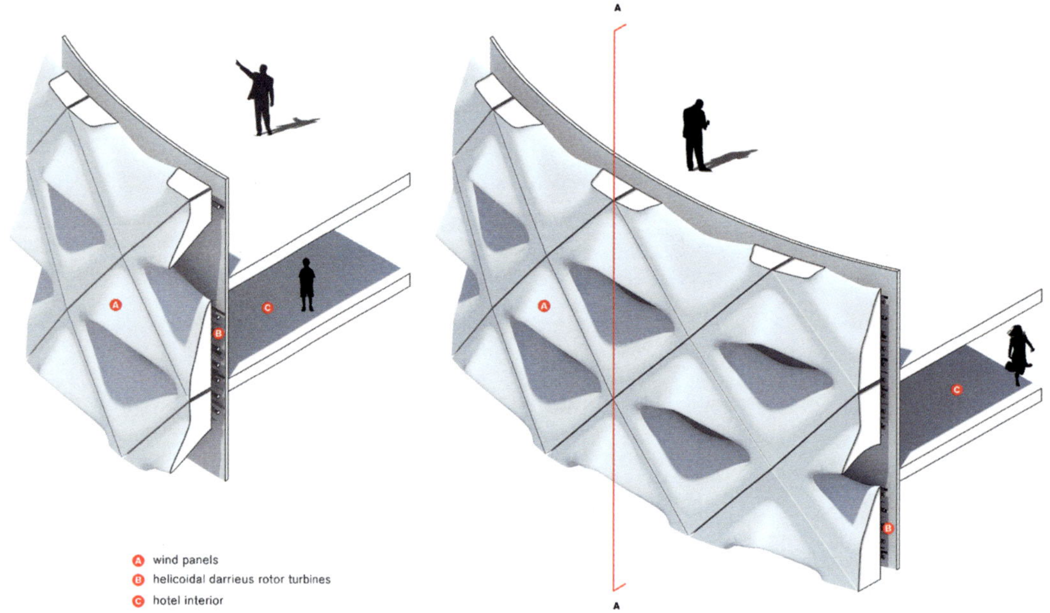

A renewable energy mechanisms are incorporated into the façade with a modular system of panels that incorporates turbines. The diameter of the openings varies in order to promote natural ventilation in parallel with the cooling system that takes advantage of rainwater harvesting.

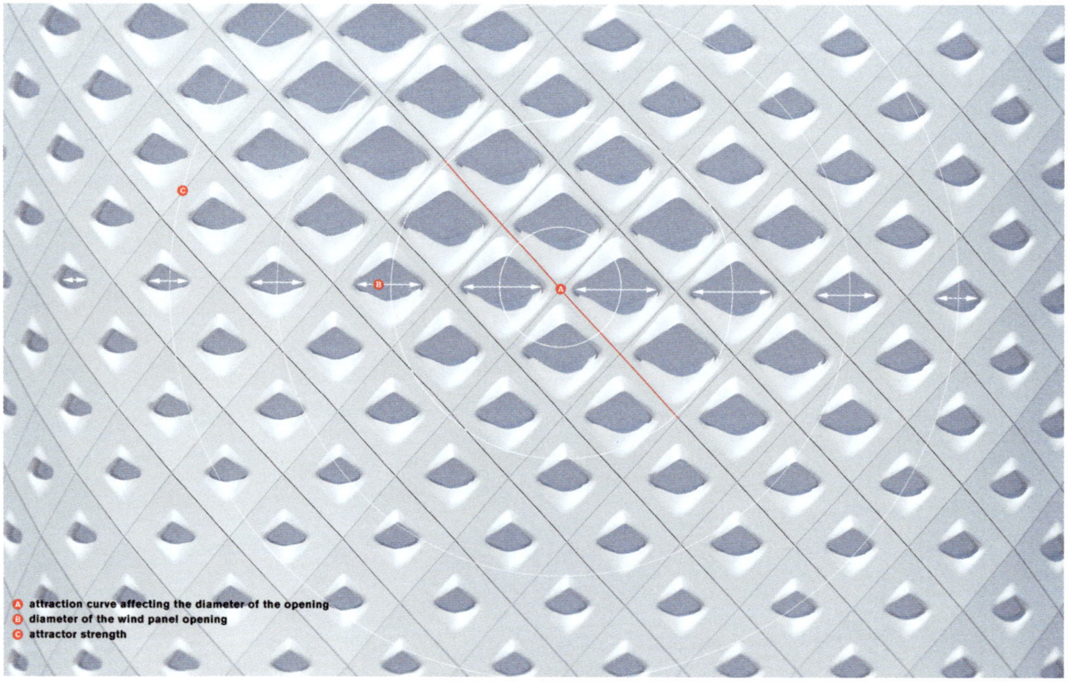

ST JOHN'S PARK PAVILION
NEW YORK

The development of a prototype for a pavilion in one of Manhattan's parks was inspired by a practical exercise exploring parametric structures that expand the possibilities of the application of this technology.

In this case, the site is a little used, central public space. The design aims to revitalize this urban void, not only through the installation of the pavilion but with a more comprehensive proposal for urban furniture and pavements that emphasize its radial structure and its geometry.

The 200 m^2 temporary pavilion incorporates a three-dimensional mesh that is coded with the coordinates and main axes on which to base the rhomboid geometry, as well as the scale of the openings in the envelope, taking as a reference the formal structure of expanded metal.

Parametric 3D Mesh Temporary

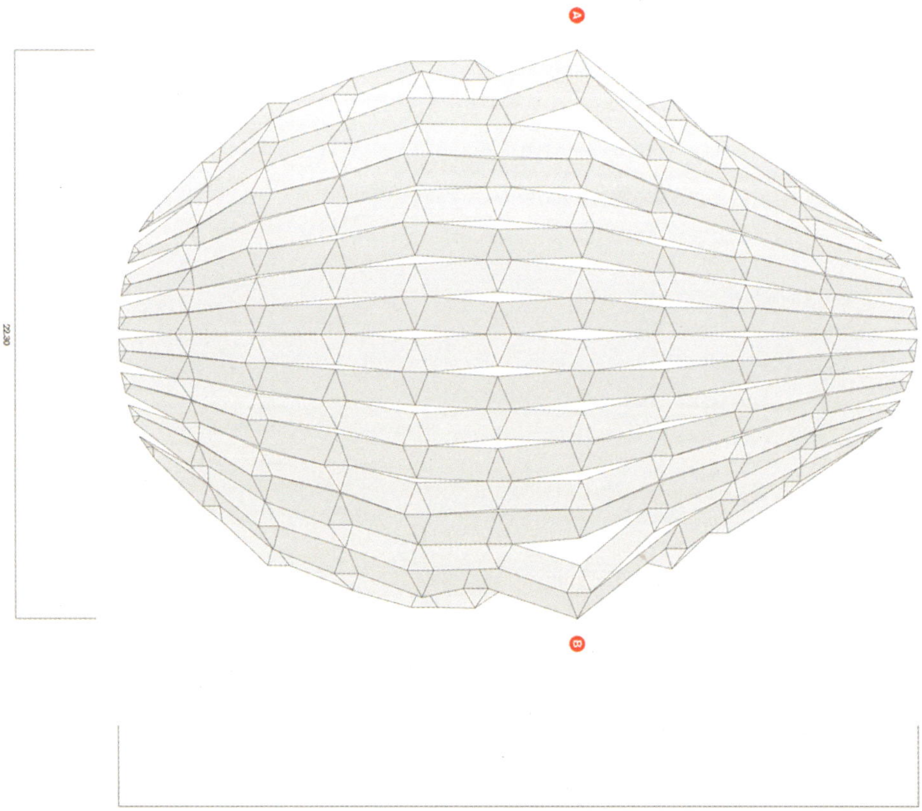

A Entrance 1

A Entrance 1
B Entrance 2

The 200m² temporary pavilion incorporates a three-dimensional mesh that is coded with the coordinates and main axes on which to base the rhomboid geometry, as well as the scale of the openings in the envelope, taking as a reference the formal structure of expanded metal.

A Entrance 1
B Entrance 2

Central Veterinary Labora
ries in Riyadh

Greenery is the main material that drives and organizes today's architectural, urban and infrastructural environments.

By including it, ON-A offers a response tied to the awareness of sustainability, while at the same time providing emotional and physical benefits to the inhabitants.

Sustainability
Bioclimatic & Efficiency

RICARDO What was the first project where you started to include vegetation as a design tool, and why did you do it?

JORDI It was for the Algeciras waterfront competition, ON-A's first competition in 2005. In fact, it was the firm's first project. Essentially, the project involved renovating a large area called the Llano Amarillo, facing the port of Algeciras, which was used as a parking area for people crossing into Morocco. The idea was to reorganize that area to give Algeciras a new public space.

The brief demanded a series of programs, including an open-air auditorium, restaurants, a small pleasure boat marina, etc. It was a very large space where we tried to generate a topography, create a ridge: at the highest point was the main road, the pedestrian path, and on both sides of the ridge, we designed different valleys to situate the different programs.

One was an uncovered parking lot, in front of that was the pleasure boat area, then an underground parking structure with a square on top of it, and an area with restaurants. Then we added programs like a children's playground, sports courts, a swimming area, an open-air auditorium and the conference center, which became a mountain that provided views toward the rock of Gibraltar.

There needed to be a building to generate that raised overlook with views of the port, the sea and the promontory in the distance. To generate the road, the paths and the valleys, we used vegetation, which we did with the company Burés. We distributed different species according to the slope, or whether they would be more or less exposed to the effects of the sea. We combined shrubs and trees depending on the program and their layout with respect to the sea and the wind. That gave us the design for the entire park. All the plants were native or Mediterranean species, with the idea of making sure the park would be sustainable, consuming a minimum of water and other resources, keeping it efficient. That was the project where it all began, where we started working with greenery as a design tool.

Green walks, sports circuits and cycle tracks constitute the initiative to transform a strategic enclave of the city into a privileged environment.

Llano Amarillo Park, Algeciras.

All the plants were native or Mediterranean species, with the idea of making sure the park would be sustainable, consuming a minimum of water and other resources, keeping it efficient.

Llano Amarillo Park, Algeciras.

The Algeciras project is directly connected with another of our projects, the park in Taichung, the second-largest city in Taiwan. The competition was for a new area of the city with various districts and a central park where the old airport used to be. We went back to this idea of greenery that tied together broad paths above the roads, in order to avoid interrupting the park. We worked with the topography, the geometry, to fit in spaces for the program and arrange them around the park, as well as a large tower that was intended as a unique building within the city: an icon.

EDUARDO The common ground with these kinds of projects is that they try to provide a solution for issues like mobility, for both vehicles and pedestrians, while looking to generate new quality urban spaces; and the idea of recycling was present in both of them. In Taichung, the project involved recycling wastewater from the canals in the area, and the project for Algeciras was intended to recycle an abandoned landscape with an outmoted seafront.

To address those problems, we tried to make greenery the main material that would drive and organize the new urban conditions. In the Llano Amarillo we generated a pattern. First we looked at the points of conflict in terms of mobility, and we tried to resolve them using green bridges: wide paths that would let the vegetation cross over. To reorganize the interior spaces, we created another Escher-like pattern, which transitions from one geometric form to another, and the program is generated within that form. That's where we added the circulation for pedestrians and bicycles.

In the end, the negative of that pattern results in a series of circulations, of optimizations that provide efficient access to all the areas of the new program that is housed in the midst of that green space. In this case, we used a Voronoi pattern which gave us control over the geometry.

In Taichung, we incorporated water recycling into the design, because two rivers run through the area, one

Taichung Gateway Park. --See page 138--

to the north and one to the south. Most of the polluted wastewater runs into the northern river, so what we did was generate a lake. The lake filters the solids from the liquid, and then that water runs down into another lake, which is much lower than the other two. As the water flows down, it gets aerated and it's purified by the vegetation, until it reaches the final lake at the lowest point. We harness the topography to provide clean water to all the park's plantlife. We also use the green bridges to create wildlife corridors.

The program is tucked into this green pattern. In Algeciras we tried to create a programmatic topography. In contrast, in Taichung, because of the project's morphology, we had to make more free-standing buildings with organic forms, like the drops of that water that are the foundation for the design's regeneration efforts.

RICARDO_ I think it's really interesting how greenery as a design material responds to an expanded ecological awareness. Where do you think that ecological awareness comes from? And how did you start incorporating it into your designs?

JORDI_ In my case, it started with my final degree project, under Alfons Soldevila. The site was the highway through Castelldefels on the coast near Barcelona, and the theme was "How buildings are perceived from cars or at high speeds"; you could choose your own program. I worked on the only section of the site where the pine forest reaches the sea, and I invented a program to preserve that space, which was used as a parking lot by weekend visitors, and organize it. So, I created a series of fractal growth units between the trees to generate a parking lot that looked random but actually followed its own set of rules. It was a unifying idea that made it possible to snake around the trees, maintaining nearly all of them. The end result was a parking lot that was created without touching the trees, adding dunes and vegetation.

There was this awareness of trying to preserve an existing natural resource while generating green spaces. It might have to do with being born in a city like Barcelona, where there really are no green spaces, and having travelled to other cities, in Germany, for example, where there's green everywhere and large parks. The amount of green space per inhabitant is much higher than what we have here. That might be one reason for the pull to design more natural spaces.

EDUARDO We're also interested in mixing green with infrastructures. Why can't a bridge be a habitable surface for the people who live on either side? My final degree project, under the same professor, was a building above a highway: a connector for mobility between the two sides, since highways tend to appear like scars across the city that limit your space, and it housed the necessary program.

JORDI I think all these ideas come together in our Nou parc project for Barcelona, which is a huge space, a real opportunity for the city. We thought, why not take advantage of that infrastructure, that huge construction to make a mountain that is a park for the city to enjoy? Right now, the Camp Nou is an island between the university campus in Zona Universitaria and the neighborhood of Les Corts, totally closed off. It doesn't contribute anything to daily life in either of those areas. It's just a barrier between them; and all it does is create problems on game days. We could take this opportunity to turn the area into a huge green space, not only to connect the neighborhoods, but also for the whole city of Barcelona to enjoy, since it could offer more than 26 hectares of green. It would be a park for the university, which currently has a concrete campus, and for Les Corts. At the same time, it would work programmatically for F.C. Barça.

EDUARDO And there are examples to look at: Frei Otto's Olympic Village in Munich is a great one. You can't tell whether you're in a park or amid stadiums. It's all integrated into the landscape. It's always full of people.

We could take this opportunity to turn the area into a huge green space, not only to connect the neighborhoods, but also for the whole city of Barcelona to enjoy, since it could offer more than 26 hectares of green.

Nou Parc, Barcelona, before and after proposal. --See page 146--

RICARDO In these three urban-scale projects, greenery is an integrating element; it's infrastructure, it's a connector, and it also guarantees sustainability in a broad sense. Now I'd be interested to hear how you incorporate vegetation on a smaller scale, in a domestic setting.

EDUARDO Having greenery nearby provides emotional and physical benefits. The idea is to take advantage of all those benefits, and that emotional place where green can take you, from the architecture itself. The idea is to live with greenery or amid greenery, as opposed to living in a house and having a garden outside. In a single-family house that's easier and more direct, but in a multi-family building it's interesting how you bring the green into the building or onto the façades. The plus that we give to the single-family homes is to generate an envelope using the greenery itself, like we did in the Green Nest House project. That envelope is an architectural material. Now we're working with the company Verdtical—specialized in green façades—and that helps us save on insulation, because we're already in compliance with the building code through the green building envelope, and it provides climatic comfort. We treat greenery as a material and as an organizer of space, in urban terms—not simply a decorative element.

RICARDO In a project for a house in Barcelona from 2019 (Loop House), you used a spiral arrangemnet that was also covered in greenery. What did the greenery contribute to that design, compared to the one you just mentioned (Green Nest House)?

JORDI The Green Nest House is more like a small cabin, a minimal house where the concept was to create a green wall toward the exterior. It was an opaque house, with privacy from the street, but then it opens up completely toward the inside of the lot. The idea of the vegetation is that it should be native to the surroundings; it should grow naturally and the maintenance should be minimal. In any environment, the vegetation would be adapted to the surroundings, so it would create a kind of camouflage. With Loop House, the idea is reversed: we take a given plot, and we want to gain the maximum surface area of green. In this case, we're talking about a programmatic green: a garden, a vegetable patch, and even an accessible roof that provides more open space. We worked with a plot where most of the surface area is occupied by the house, so we put the vegetable garden on top. The spiral shape is a way to keep the house fully connected, with a continuous path from the ground floor up to the roof.

Green Nest House.

Green Nest House is more like a small cabin, a minimal house where the concept was to create a green wall toward the exterior.

Zero Emissions
Energy Efficiency
Green Camouflage
Healthy

100% of the weight of the Green Nest House is made with healthy materials.

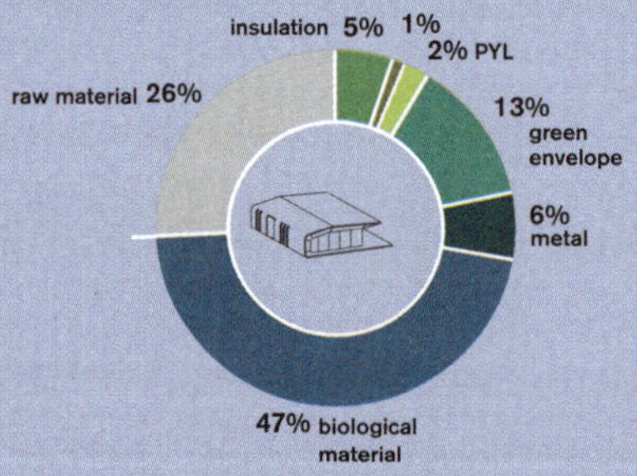

28% of materials are recycled.

47% of materials are biological.

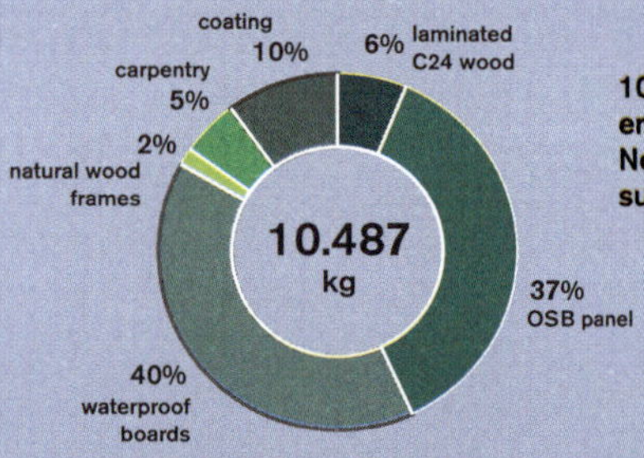

100% of the wood employed at the Green Nest House comes from sustainable forests.

MINIMAL CARBON FOOTPRINT

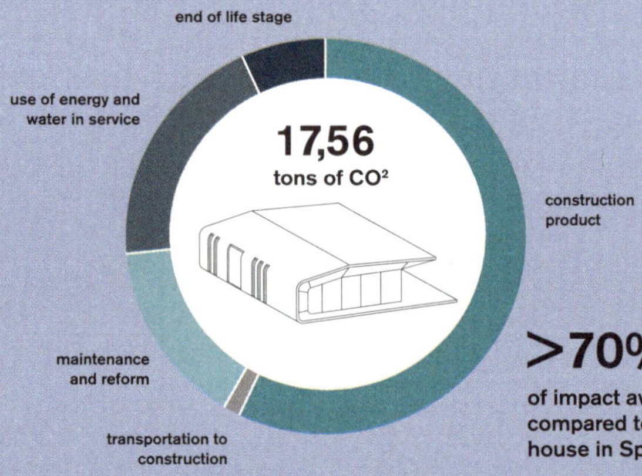

>70%

of impact avoided compared to a traditional house in Spain.

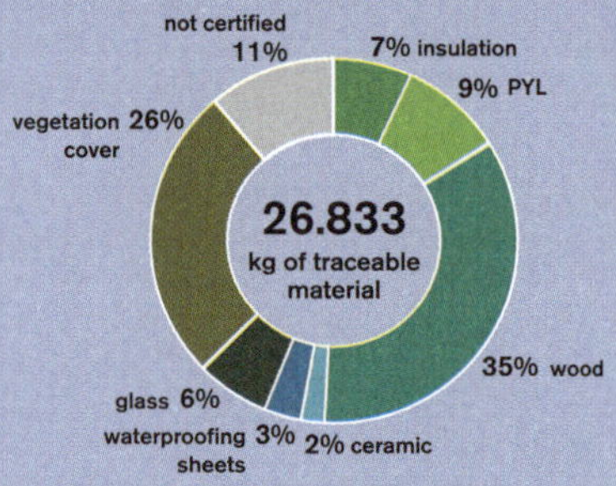

89% of the weight of Green Nest House is made with certified and traceable materials

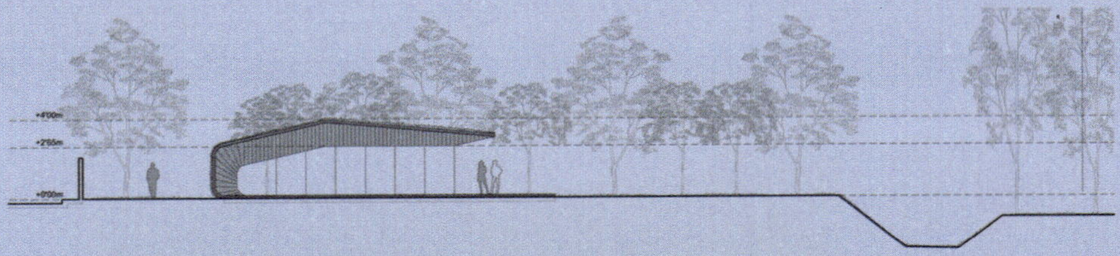

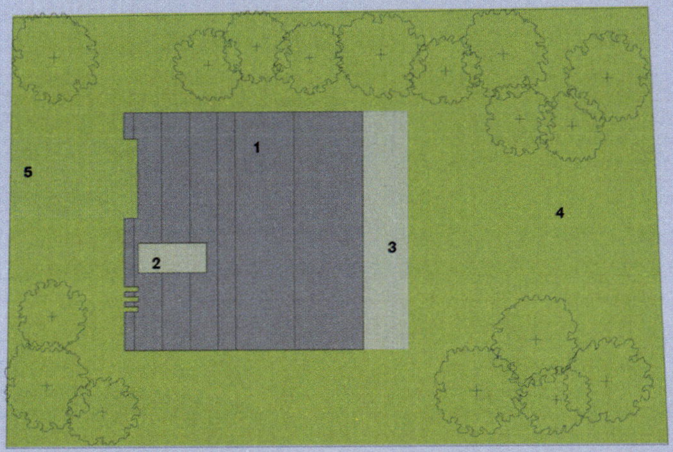

1 Roof
2 Patio
3 Terrace
4 Garden
5 Entrance

Model A

2 rooms + parking

Model B

3 rooms

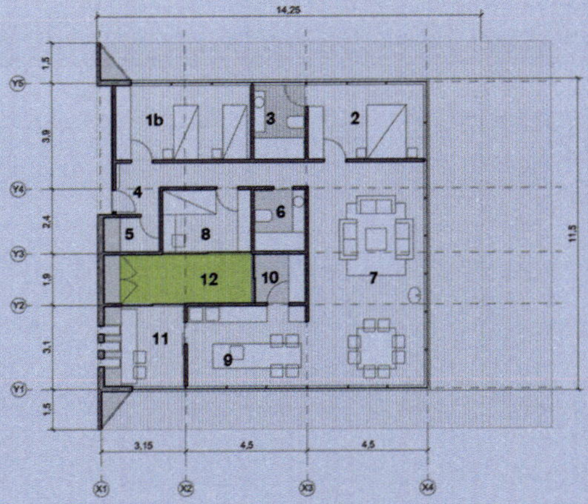

1a garage
1b double room
2 main room
3 main bathroom
4 acces
5 facilities room
6 bath-room
7 living/dinning room
8 guests room
9 kitchen
10 laundry
11 workshop
12 patio

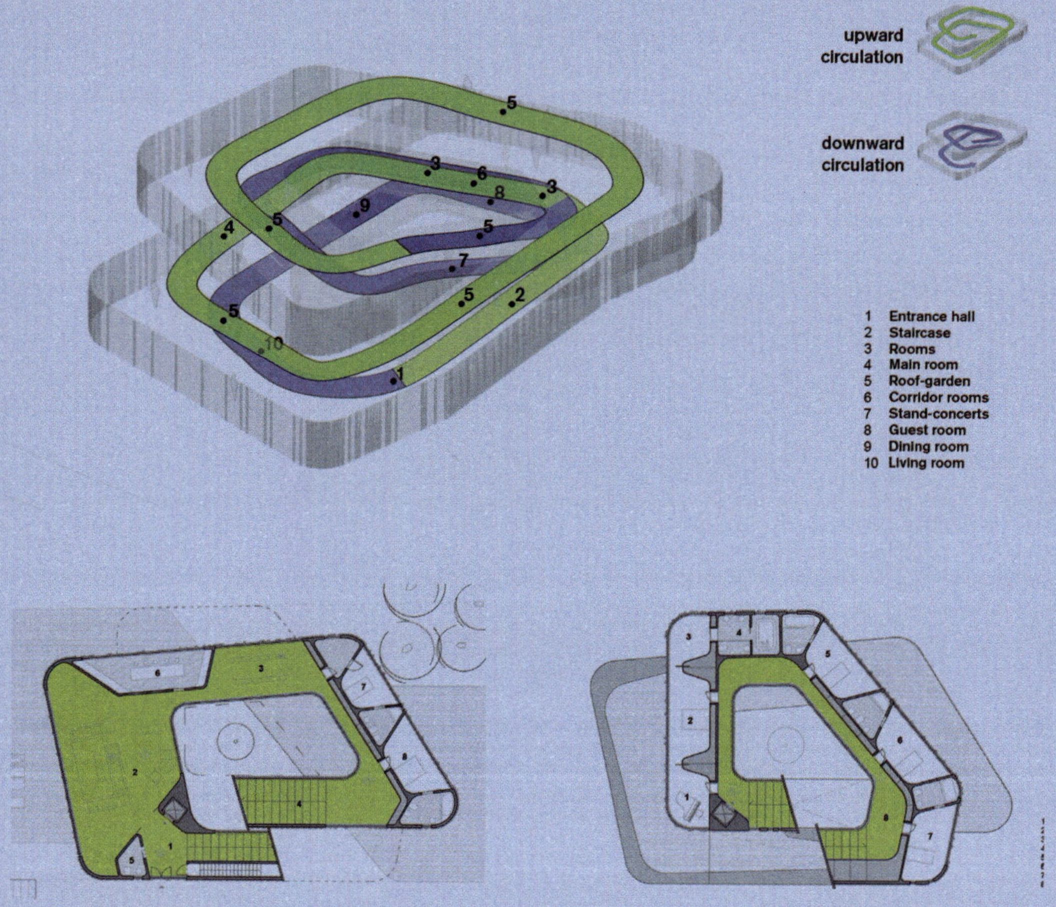

Loop House, Barcelona.

RICARDO I'd like to hear a little more about your collaboration with Verdtical. How does an architecture firm decide to bring in these consultants or experts and work with greenery as a design tool?

EDUARDO Essentially, for the technical aspects and for the reality of it. As architects, we know about the benefits and we know how to handle the material, but in the end you need the data and the professional experience in a very specific emerging sector. We're still in the early stages of treating greenery as a material and being able to measure the benefits in a quantifiable way. In that regard, we're already working with sensors to understand how plants recycle the harmful microparticles released by the construction materials themselves, as well as the particles in the enviroment. We want to systematize and protocolize all this, so that it's ultimately buildable. We want to demonstrate that, in a house with a green roof, the inhabitants will be breathing less CO_2 than their next-door neighbors.

JORDI As for our collaboration with Verdtical, we've sought out technological partners from the very beginning. We're architects, of course, we have our intuitions, our ideas, but we need to surround ourselves with professionals who are capable of carrying them out. Just like we have collaborators for structural engineering or building facilities, we know that if we want to use greenery we need to surround ourselves with companies that really know about it.

RICARDO Why is Verdtical, a company that works with greenery as a material, interested in collaborating with architects?

JORDI They realized that our firm has been working along these lines from the beginning. It started with the Algeciras Park in 2005. Then there was the competition to expand the Lleida-Alguaire airport, in 2010, continuing the green of the fields, generating strips of vegetation. There was a hotel project in Olot from 2010, where the reference was to generate a building that evoked the image of the Croscat volcano, a green mountain with a reddish interior. And then the 2011 Taichung Project, which we talked about before, and a high-rise for Taipei from 2013.

In this case, we're talking about a programmatic green: a garden, a vegetable patch, and even an accessible roof that provides more open space.

Loop House, Barcelona.

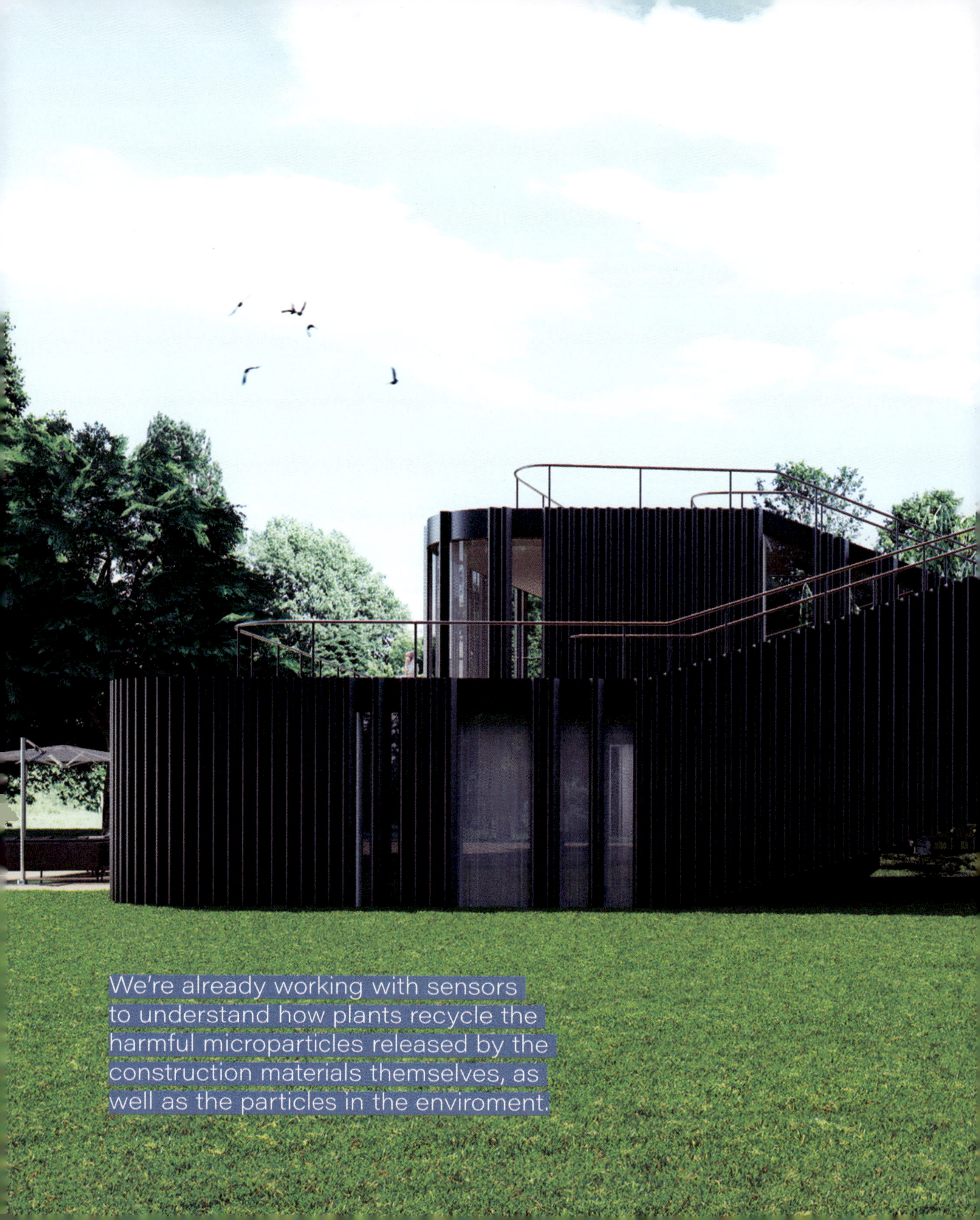

We're already working with sensors to understand how plants recycle the harmful microparticles released by the construction materials themselves, as well as the particles in the enviroment.

Loop House, Barcelona.

RICARDO In that last project, did you look into the pros and cons of what it means to use vegetation in tall buildings?

JORDI As for the benefits, they're the same ones we've already mentioned. The height brings in a technical question: how to water the plants efficiently. In Taiwan, the irrigation would be 10% of what would be needed in Spain, since it's a very humid place. There would be a structural

Taichung Gateway Park. **--See page 138--**

issue because of the weight and the wind. The terraces are wider because you need areas for soil or substrates. We don't look at those things as cons, though; they're technical questions and, therefore, they can be resolved.

RICARDO So, do you think that's a clear evolution in architecture, using vegetation in section, as in some contemporary cases like Boeri or Fujimoto?

JORDI It's also a question of vision on the level of architectural production. In other words, the same building works without the plants, but adding them provides extra benefits for the people who'll be living in it. It filters the light, for example. As opposed to using architectural elements, we can extend the overhangs and add vegetation. The function is the same, but the method is different. There aren't any seasonal cycles in Taiwan, so it would always be green. It's also important to think about how the building's appearance changes depending on the time of year. You can have green in spring and summer. In autumn, when the leaves are falling, you have to work out how they're collected, but there's got to be a technical solution for that. In winter, you get more sunlight, which is when you need it, and in spring the cycle starts all over again. It's a question of looking at nature, which has been evolving over thousands of years, and thinking about how we can take advantage of this natural knowledge and incorporate it into buildings.

RICARDO Have you designed any projects where the vegetation, along with climatological and emotional benefits, also produces food?

JORDI We did it on a small scale with the Green Tiger, a restaurant in Barcelona, which ultimately wasn't developed, but the idea was to build a green wall where it was part agriculture, part show-cooking.

The idea was to build a green wall where it was part agriculture, part show-cooking.

The Green Tiger Restaurant, Barcelona.

We're also looking at the possibilities in inhabitable structures, in the context of city development. We're talking about how to inhabit the Earth in a sustainable and efficient way.

We have hyper saturated cities that are becoming increasingly denser, whereas there's a huge part of the Earth that is inhabited or poorly inhabited.

In Spain, there is an interior agricultural area that is full of towns with somewhere between 20 and 200 inhabitants, and that generates a network of connecting roads and infrastructures, which results in unsustainable consumption and mobility patterns. **So we created a self-sufficient building/city concept: with its own farming setup and waste recycling.** This is the first time in history that we have the ability to inhabit any place on the planet at high density due to technology, since we can capture energy anywhere, whether its solar, or wind, the tides, or geothermal energy.

We can travel fast and efficiently over long distances. Hyperloop-type projects are already showing that we can reach ground speeds of 1,000 km/h efficiently without any large infrastructure. Drones let us cross over virgin territories without needing to exploit them or generate road networks that destroy them. There are quite a few projects, for example, in Africa, to create drone ports to replace expensive and inefficient infrastructures that eventually deteriorate due to harsh weather. Drones can deliver medicine, food...

With this new mobility, and in connection with pay-per-use technology, people won't need private vehicles anymore. We've also increased our ability to recycle our own waste or to grow food in any kind of environment or to generate recyclable materials. If we can create it and bring it into this building, so it is consumed, recycled, and generates energy again, and the building doesn't end up generating exterior waste, then we can have towers to house 1,000, 2,000 or 5,000 people in the middle of a forest, a mountain, or the Arctic, and the footprint will be as small as possible in every way.

We can have towers to house 1,000, 2,000 or 5,000 people in the middle of a forest, a mountain, or the Arctic, and the footprint will be as small as possible in every way.

Hermeticity.

Hermeticity is an experimental
study towards colonizing extreme
environments with a reduced footprint.

RICARDO When you incorporate greenery, in some way, you're shifting the classical typologies of architecture. In an urban environment, the infrastructure becomes a park. In single-family homes, the roof becomes an extension of the ground. And with towers, someting similar happens; they become more efficient autonomous entities. Aside from the benefits we've been talking about, greenery also goes hand-in-hand with innovation in the spatial and programmatic conceptualization of these projects. For example, what was your approach for the Windmill Towers just outside Barcelona, from 2013?

JORDI That project originated with the idea of generating a high-density development in a wooded environment. We were looking to minimize the buildings' footprint, which actually disappears in the satellite view, so that we would have the towers, the underground parking structure, and the paths through the woods that connect them.

The communal spaces appear on the roof, where there are swimming pools, grassy leisure areas, and a solar collection area. We wanted a high-rise building, but with houses; that's why the units are duplexes. In a conventional single-family home you have the living room, the kitchen, and the day area on the ground floor, and then the bedrooms are on the second floor. You generate large terraces. Whereas, here, we designed a garden in section, while maintaining privacy. That's why we used the blade geometry, rotated sequentially, giving us those tall heights above each of the gardens.

You never have that feeling of a balcony: the next built level above you is at a height of 12 meters, so you have full sun, air, ventilation. If the development had been designed with isolated single-family homes, it would cover the entire area, with streets in between, each with its own pool, etc. The forest would have been destroyed.

EDUARDO This way, we give everyone all the benefits of a single-family home, but with a minimal footprint. In terms of sustainability, we don't just try to use more efficient building services and materials; there's also efficiency in terms of the program and the geometry of the architecture itself. Here we're minimizing the land use, which has an impact on conserving the fauna and the flora in the surroundings.

Windmill Towers, Barcelona.

Ultimately, it has to do with the optimization of space. It's much more efficient to have 20 houses in section than 20 houses in a row, when it comes to recycling waste, grey water, biomass. Here, using restraint and precision, the benefits are amazing. To some extent, it's a reading of what happens in cities.

Energy is generated at a distance of 50 km, waste disposal is 100 km away, food comes from at least 100 km away. In order to bring in all these materials and this energy for consumption, you need infrastructures and you have to burn fuel. As an alternative, we can rethink the very conception of the architecture from the beginning.

Windmill Towers, Barcelona.

In terms of sustainability, we don't just try to use more efficient building services and materials; there's also efficiency in terms of the program and the geometry of the architecture itself.

JORDI We tried out a similar exercise, with a different geometry, for the Europan competition in Sweden. The site was in a flood zone, and we proposed the same concept of houses that revolve around an axis, generating a topography so that they are elevated above sea level. We took advantage of the existing roads to generate the cells that attach to them, so we avoided having to develop any new roads.

RICARDO I'd like to hear about the Neom project, from 2018. There's a typological paradigm shift, where you combine this relationship between geometry and form, with material and energy efficiency.

EDUARDO With Neom they asked us for a "smart city", but what is a smart city? I can make a smart city with all the conceptual landmarks, but it may occupy acres and acres of land. Why don't we put all that program and its inhabitants into a much smaller space? If we do, everything will be better, because the connections between users will be much more efficient. Ideally, the user should be 15 minutes from everything: in terms of resources, in terms of the distribution of materials, and in terms of climate efficiency within the city. The more surface area there is, the more inefficient the climate control is, because you have more losses in both cold and heat.

What we looked at with the Neom project was: instead of generating a master plan and then putting efficient buildings into it, why don't we make a very efficient master plan that contains buildings? That gave rise to the Neom concept, which is a cell that contains everything and is replicable.

Imagine a system so effective that it is efficient in any environment, as hostile as it may be: a desert or the poles. The only thing you need to connect with the outside are very precise accesses, which can use a hyperloop or drone technology. We could have different self-sufficient islands within the same extended environment.

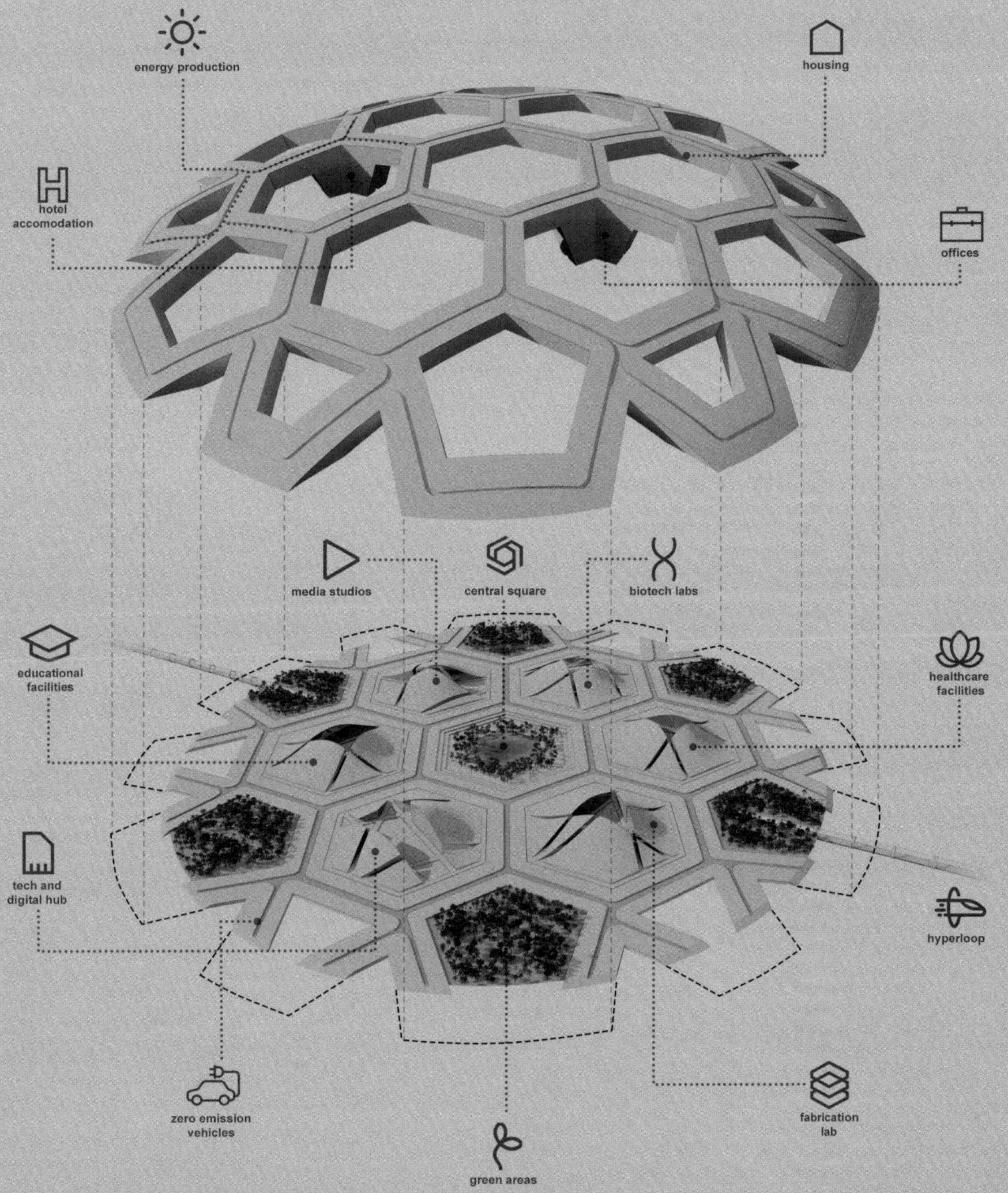

Neom City, Saudi Arabia.

--See page 304--

What we proposed was a master plan where the geometric distribution for accessing the buildings and the different interrelationships in the city are formed by the buildings themselves. At the same time, given the site conditions (an area with a lot of sun exposure), we imagined that all the buildings would protect themselves as much as possible against this condition in the surroundings. So we created the dome, which is a dome-shield-building that also collects solar energy, and which feeds back into the city itself and protects its inhabitants by creating a microclimate inside.

JORDI_ Again, we relied on geometry to resolve the program and all the requirements: in this case, for a city in the middle of the desert, in a hostile territory. There's a dome shape that generates a shield. Instead of having exposed buildings, we develop a shield that protects us, which affects the geometry of the buildings, turning them inward, and, as a result, their sun exposure is minimized. This protective shield is used to capture solar energy on all its south-facing surfaces, and at the same time it generates an oasis microclimate. It has a footprint, but we minimize the buildable area.

EDUARDO_ Then there's the program itself within the dome that needs to be in contact with the ground. So, what happens there? The dunes, the hills that emerge, also house parts of the program.

RICARDO_ Earlier on, we talked about the benefits of greenery, in terms of the psychological and emotional impact. The greenery helps you determine forms or geometries and materials; it leads to invention or innovation in typologies. To what extent does the greenery also add a layer in emotional terms?

EDUARDO_ We've always looked to nature itself as a reference. Our first project, the 5 Sentidos Lounge Bar, from 2005,

5 Sentidos Lounge Bar, Girona.
--See Page 64--

emerged from the analysis of how to generate a space using a single material, but which is also very unique. Natural structures are an inspiration for us. In this case, specifically, we looked at a bone cell. If you look at it under a microscope, it's a series of spaces in a single material. Having that reference to nature has also led us toward transmitting that emotion through greenery. Like adding one more layer of complexity to the architecture, but in a very controlled way. You have an attractive overall geometry, but if you go into more detail, you see a green environment that also has its own geometry. So, you start making combinations, making sure everything meshes. If you look at the façade of a standard or traditional building, you've got the façade with a solid and empty opening. So, this is the next step. Wherever you add green material, your perception of things changes.

We're also thinking of introducing fauna, because we can host life aside from just the human inhabitants. In the end, it generates emotion; it's inescapable, like what happens to you in the middle of a forest. You can end up creating that naturalization in an urban environment; that's what gives you the emotional effect.

The Barcelona Port Area is mostly private and current logistics and tourism activities do not facilitate the use of citizens, as it is an artificial barrier.

Barcelona Port Area in the present.

New geometry will allow spaces to be transformed into greener, more democratic and diversified areas, generating resources for the port that will revert to improving the environment sustainability.

A versatile perimeter is proposed and adapted to a new layout of the spaces allowing activities of leisure, cultural, restoration, and administrative that enrich the daily life of the port and the citizens who visit it.

Proposal for remodeling the water front of Barcelona.

BIOTECH TOWER
TAIPEI

This 39-story tower of luxury homes was designed for the city of Taipei, in an area facing the Tamsui River that is undergoing an urban transformation. The façade, a large structural mesh, colors the landscape green and provides a large, glazed surface so that all the rooms can maintain a connection with the outside.

Using bioarchitecture, we designed a green building to connect the inhabitants with nature, although they are living in an urban area. In psychology, green is associated with relaxation, harmony and freshness. The design for this building aims to convey a feeling of wellbeing and health to its inhabitants and throughout its overall surroundings.

In addition to reducing the environmental impact of the construction and improving the citizens' quality of life, the building's greenery supports an emotional interaction with the end user. A green strip is designed around the perimeter of each story, which helps to distance users from the built limit, thus providing a greater sense of safety.

The interior of this 150-meter-high tower is organized to house various uses: on the ground floor there is a large lobby that provides access to the rest of the building; the next three floors are occupied by the residential club; the fourth floor through the 35th accommodate three different types of housing; and beginning from level 36 (129.70 m) there is a leisure area for users with a gym, swimming pool and restaurant.

The uniqueness of the design works as a catalyst for positive emotions: physical and visual wellbeing, comfort with sustainable materials that actively contribute to the occupants' health, and flexibility in the uses of the designed spaces.

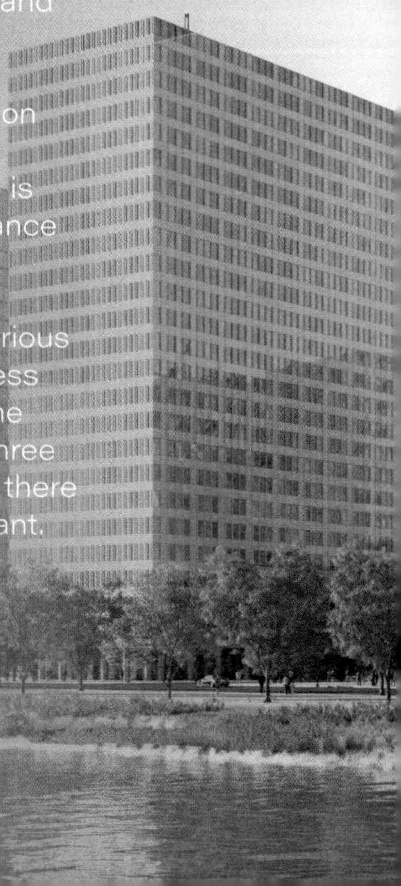

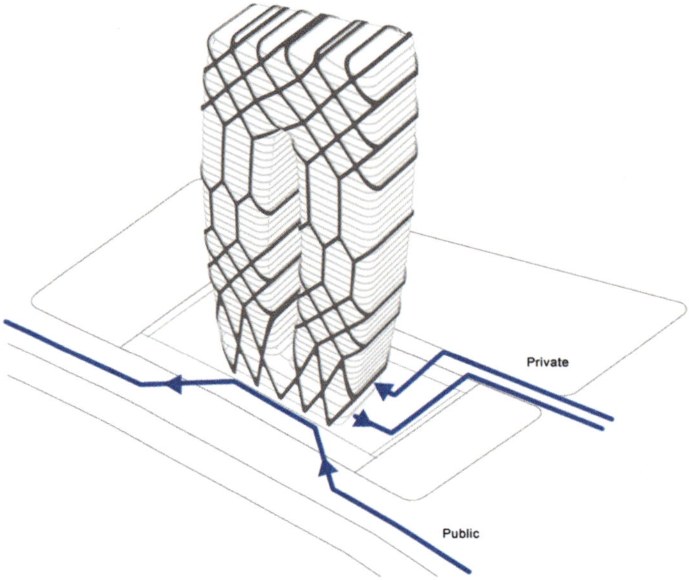

Cars circulation

Bioarchitecture Structural Mesh Well-being

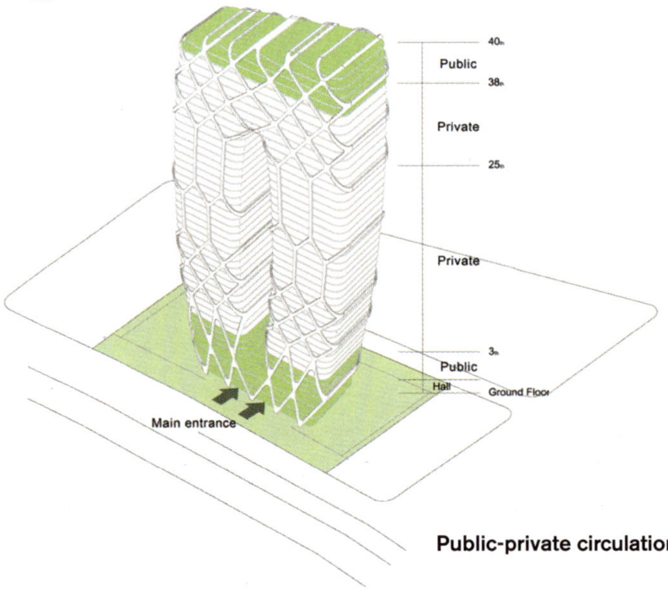

Public-private circulation

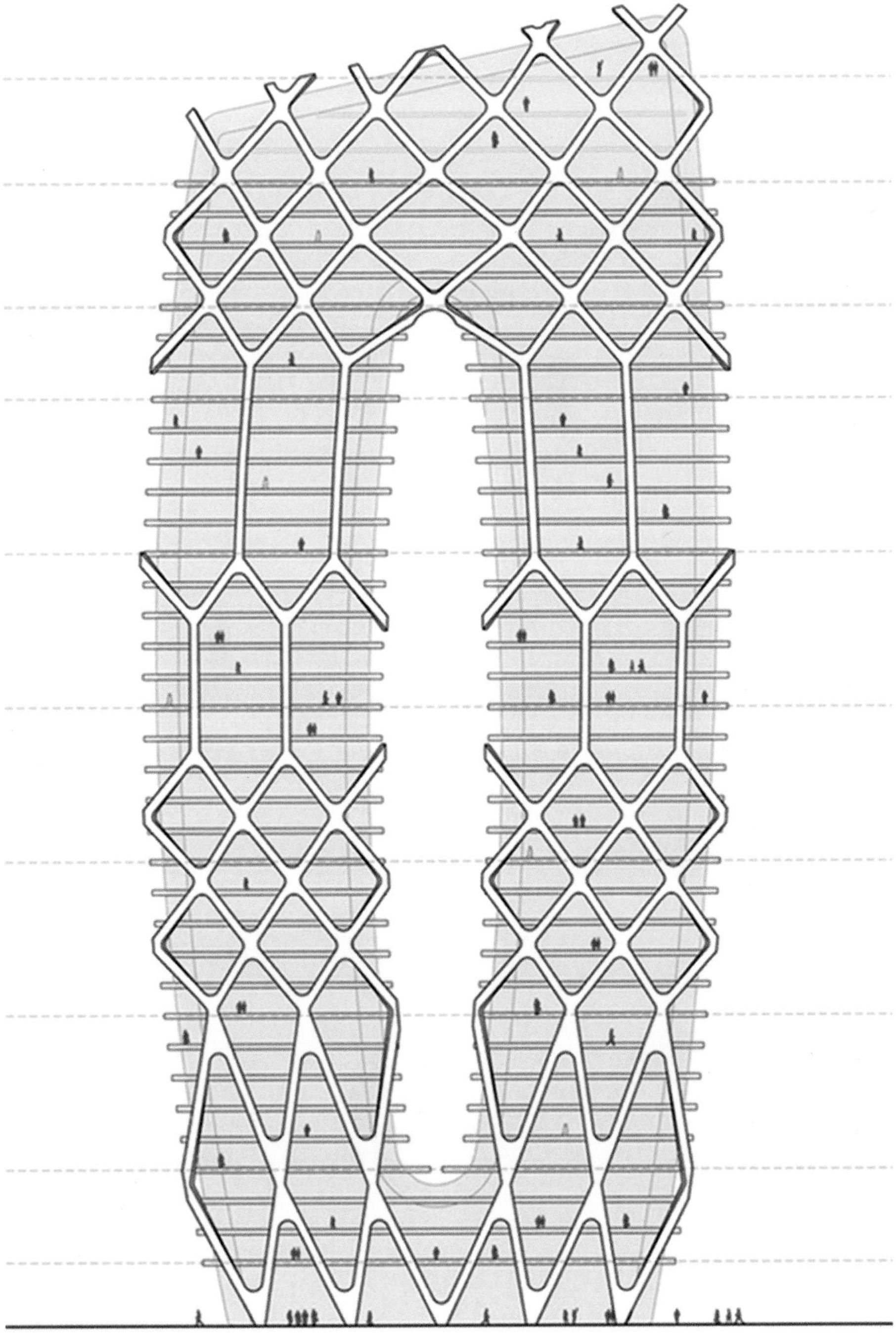

Elevation plan

The façade is a layer of technological green that appeals to sustainability from materiality, management and maintenance.

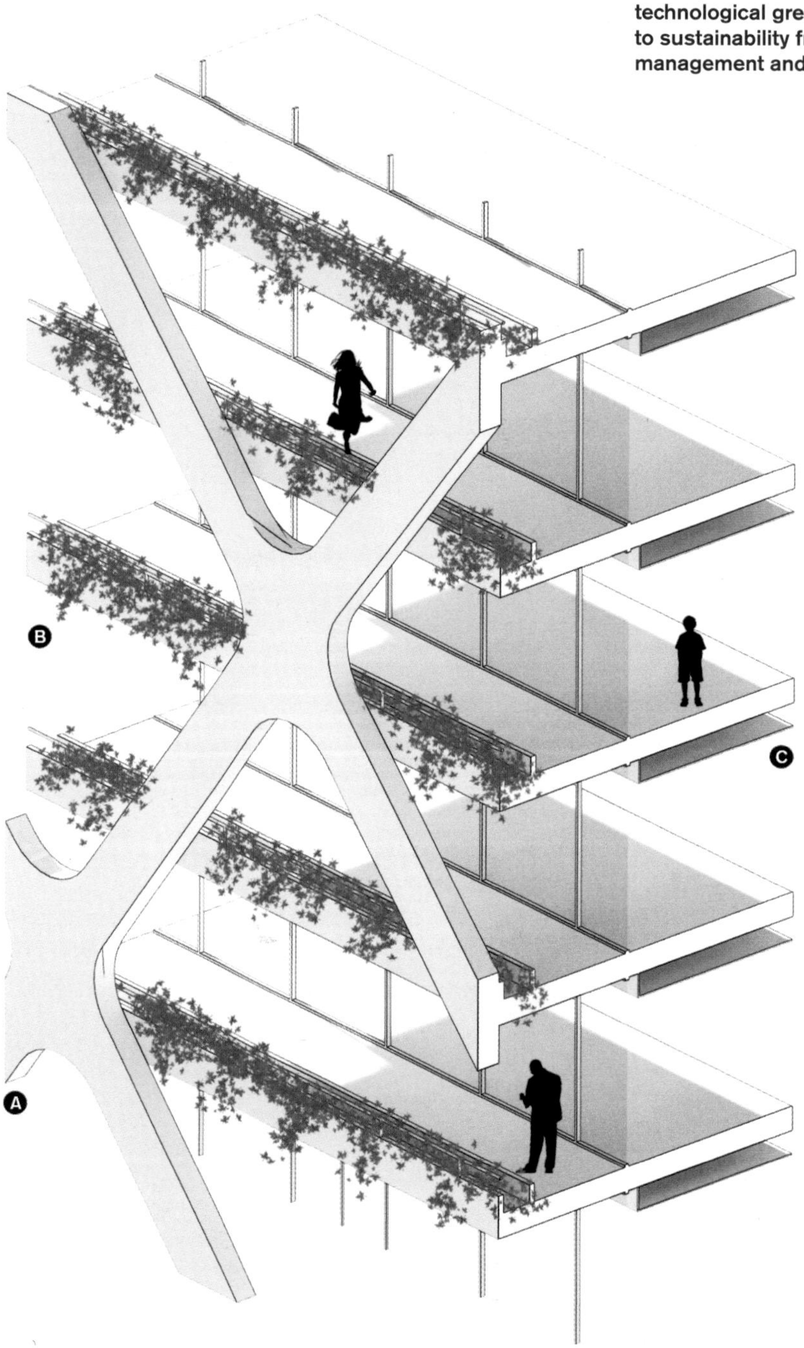

A frame structure

B slab floor

C vegetation

The interior works as a catalyst for positive emotions: physical-visual well-being, comfort with sustainable materials are factors that actively contribute to the health of its inhabitants.

The tower seeks to re-naturalize the city to reconnect people with the natural environment and thus favour the balance of ecosystems.

TAICHUNG GATEWAY PARK
TAICHUNG

A network of facilities and green areas is devised to serve as a large-scale urban park. They are articulated by a simple system of pedestrian walkways crossing over roads that have been moved underground, guaranteeing visual and spatial continuity for an area covering more than 200,000 square meters.

In Taichung, the city government is planning an urban development zone incorporating five districts responding to different profiles (financial, technological, residential and cultural). The Taichung Gateway Park international competition is the kickoff in the development of this large area of land, which will be the "green lung" for the surroundings and will help structure it and offer connections for pedestrian flows.

This design aims to give top priority to the "green" elements, ensuring their continuity by placing secondary priority on the roads that pass underneath. The area will become a huge mass of vegetation, where water and trees take center stage. It will serve as the entryway to the three public buildings that are included in the program: the Taichung City Cultural Center, the Taichung Movie City, and the brand-new Taiwan Tower, which, at 300 meters tall, will become a new landmark for the city.

In this way, sustainability, urban planning and architecture interact in a balance across an extensive area of wild forests, in which a large activity infrastructure aims to generate a new paradigm for the city.

Various analyses have served as the foundation for structuring the current program around a network of vehicle and pedestrian routes that articulate the city's districts with the green areas and lakes from the Gateway Park through a series of platforms that are directly associated with recreational and sports activities.

The proposal seeks to give top priority to green by giving it continuity to the "detriment" of the roads that pass underneath.

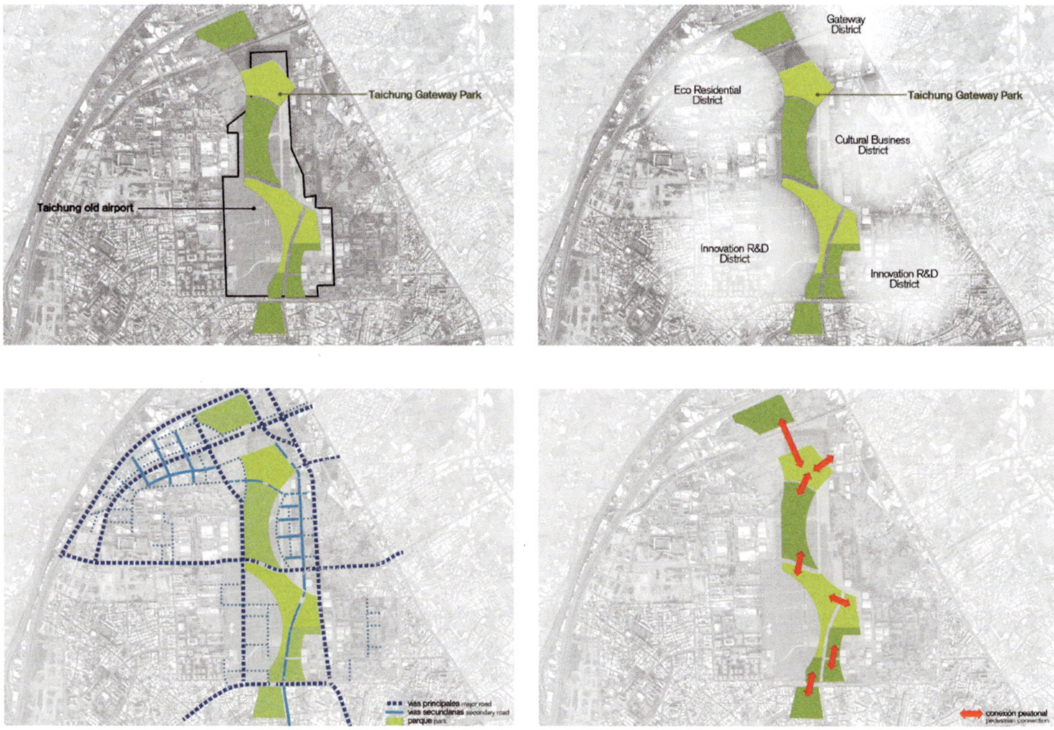

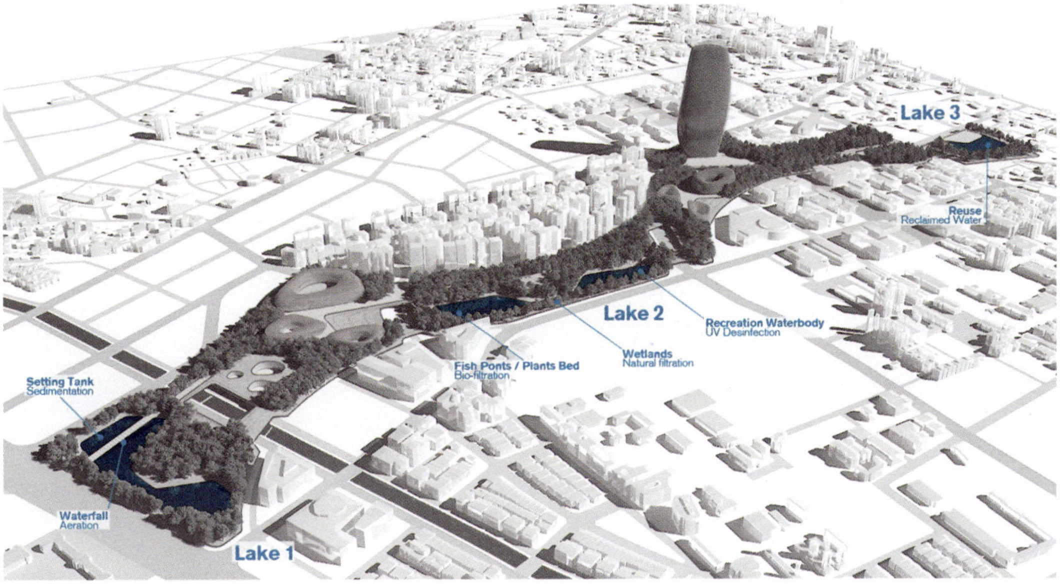

A great green lung, a network of facilities and green areas articulated under a simple scheme of pedestrian walks that overlap the now buried tracks.

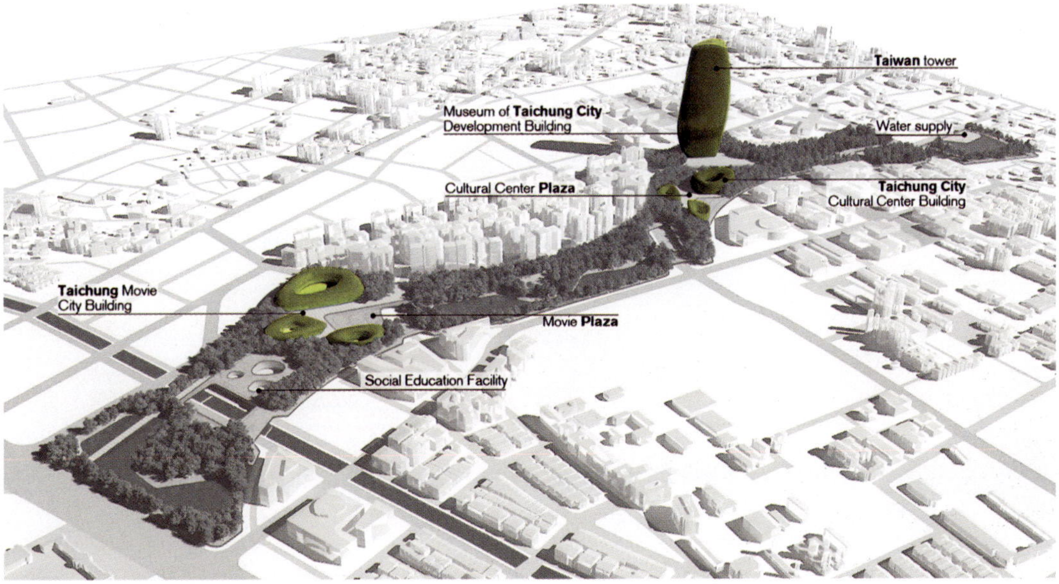

Green Lung Plant Mass Network Continuity

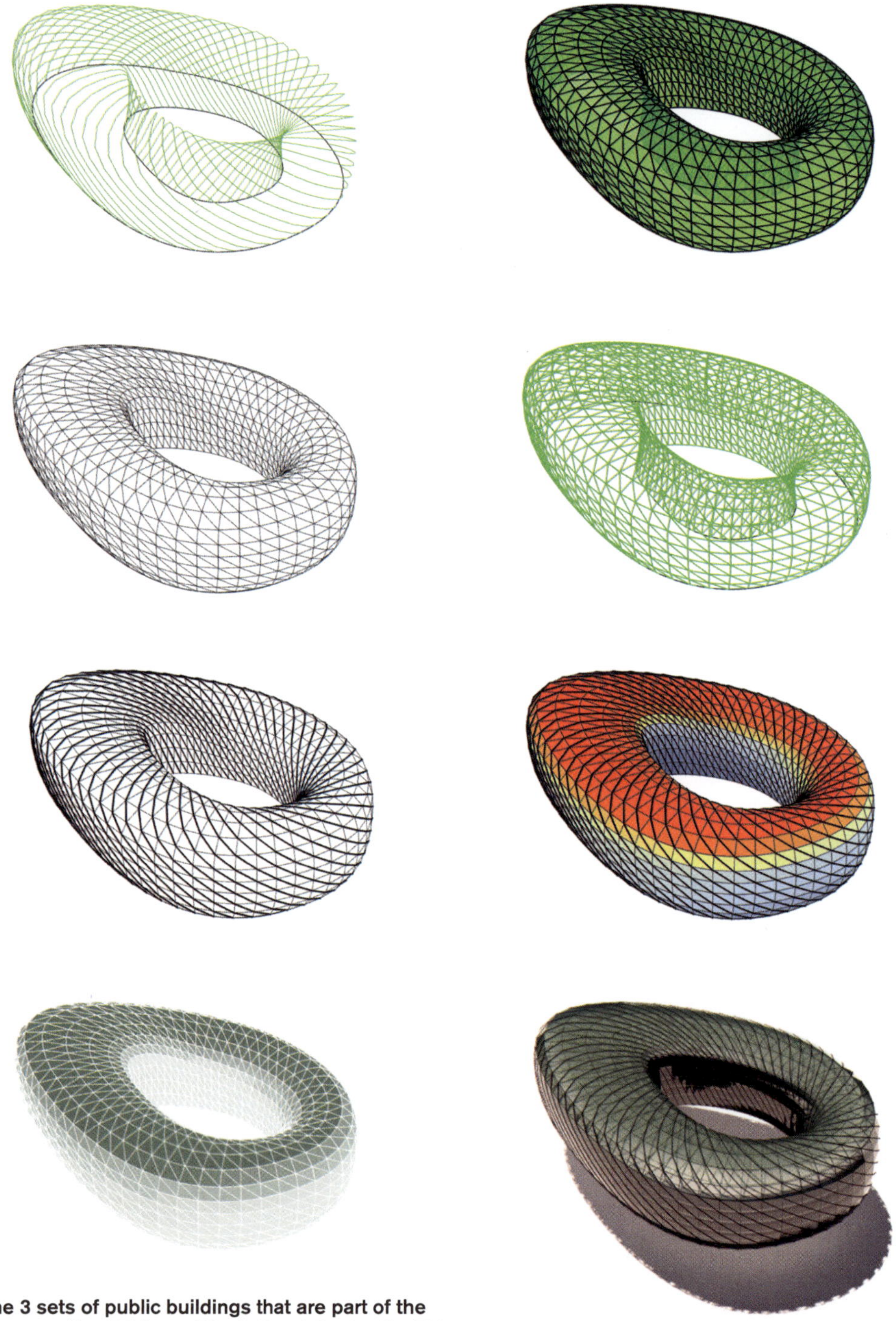

The 3 sets of public buildings that are part of the program (the Taichung City Cultural Center, the Taichung Movie City and the brand-new Taiwan Tower) become the new landmark of the city.

Sustainability, urban planning and architecture interact in a balanced way in an extensive surface of wild forests.

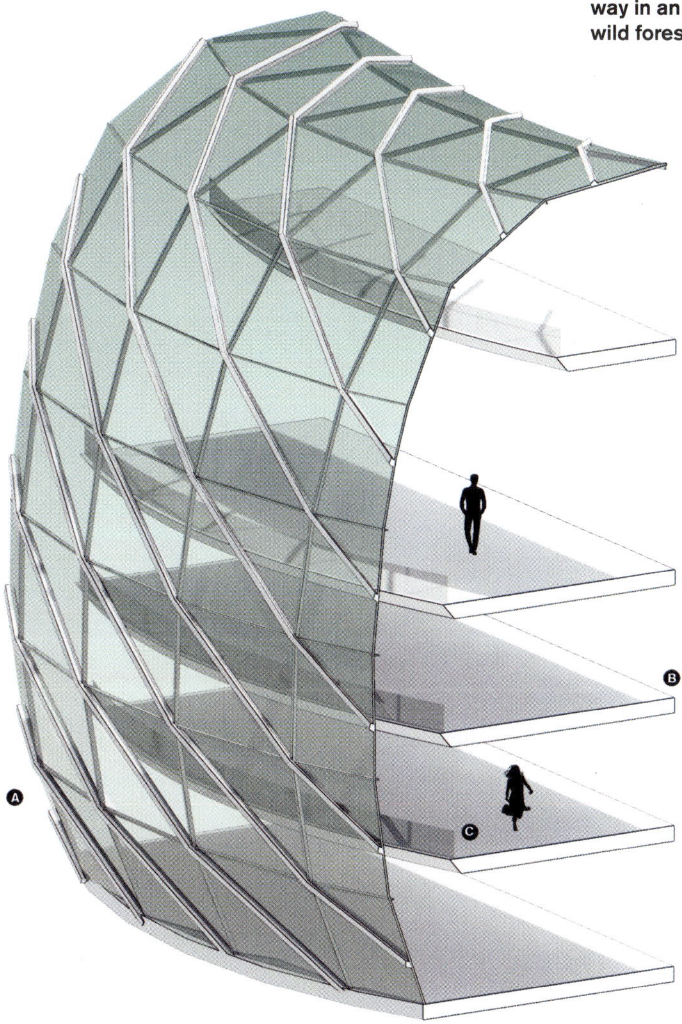

- **A** frame structure
- **B** slab floor
- **C** glass railing

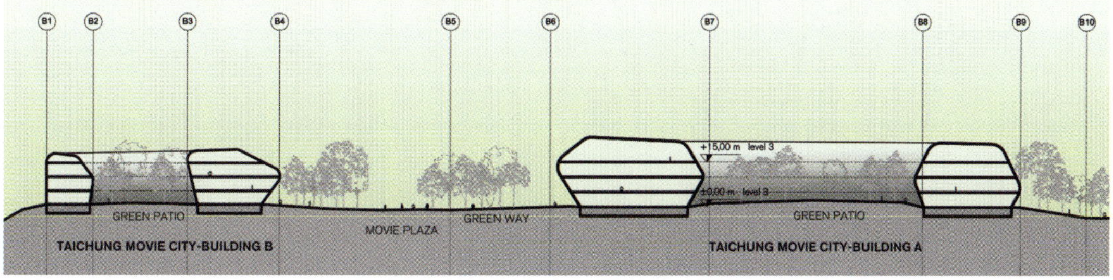

NOU PARC BARCELONA

The Nou parc project transforms the area of Barcelona's Camp Nou into an urban park.

Barcelona currently has just over 6 m^2 of green space per inhabitant. According to the WHO (World Health Organization), cities should have a minimum of 9 m^2. The Nou parc project for a wooded area intended to cover the Camp Nou in Barcelona aims to turn the area into a "green lung" for the city, using bioarchitecture as a strategy for renaturalization.

Currently, the area is a closed-off expanse of concrete. As a result, it generates an "island" effect, cutting off two large neighborhoods from one another. The space is enormous and remains unused most of the time, except during sporting events or for private tours of the facilities.

Repurposing the area would represent a great opportunity for the city of Barcelona. It would generate a new green space to connect two neighborhoods while producing 15,000 kg of oxygen/day and absorbing 25,000 kg of $C0_2$/day.

People would be able to walk or run along a 2.4 km path through the woods, relax in the landscaped areas or have a picnic, in addition to taking in a 360o panoramic view from the highest point in the park, around the edges of the stadium. The two lakes would help reduce temperatures and maintain the area, as well as serving as natural collectors for rainwater, which could be reused for irrigation and park upkeep.

The project propose a forest that would cover the Camp Nou, to turn the area into a great green lung using bioarchitecture as a strategy for renaturation.

Barcelona would gain a new green space capable of connecting neighborhoods while producing 15,000kg oxygen/day and absorb 25,000kg of CO_2 / day.

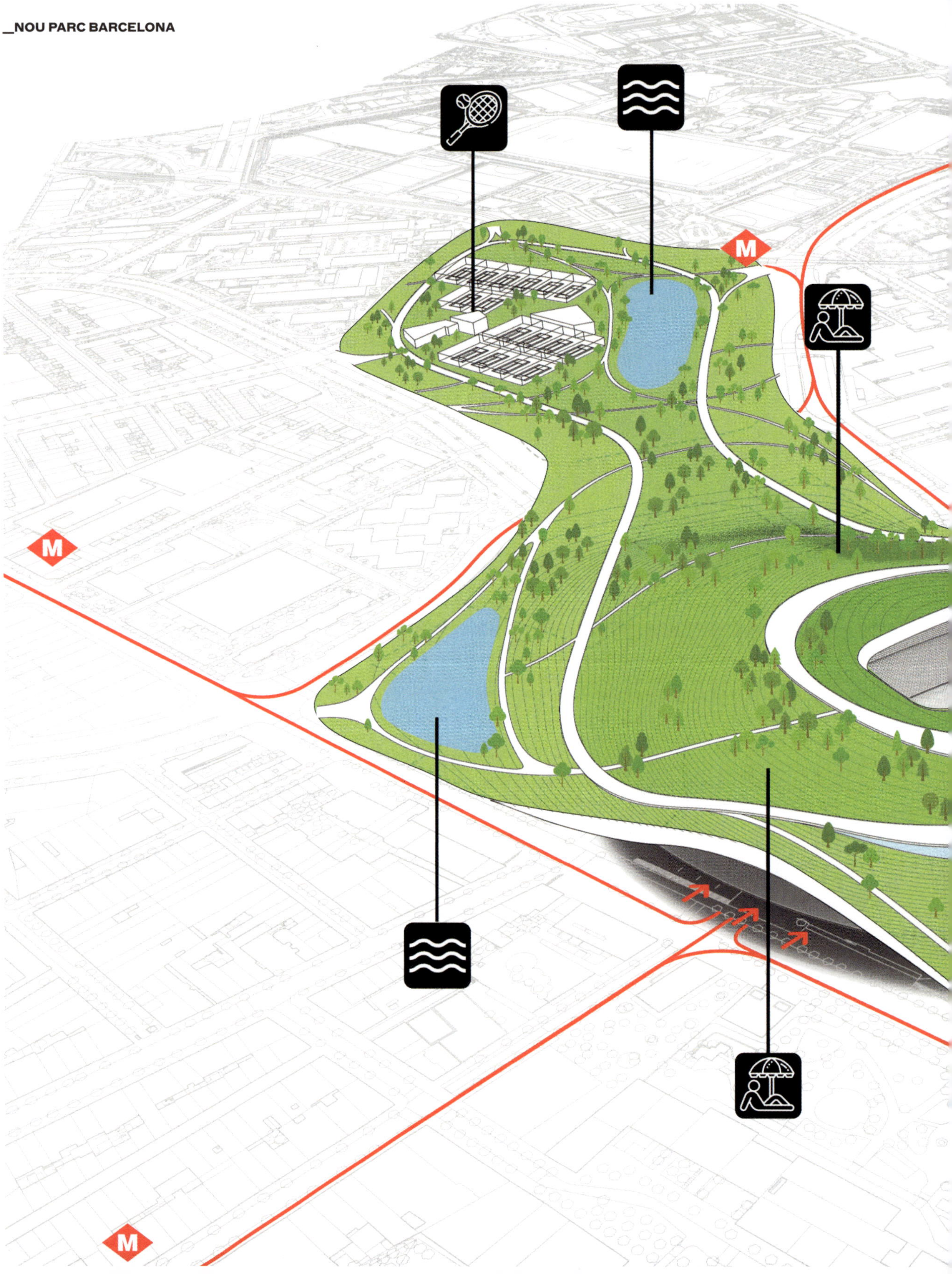
M
M
M

M
M
M
M

Raising the topography and creating a blanket of green forest above the stadium and its facilities, Nou Parc project shows how nature would come back to cities without losing buildable space.

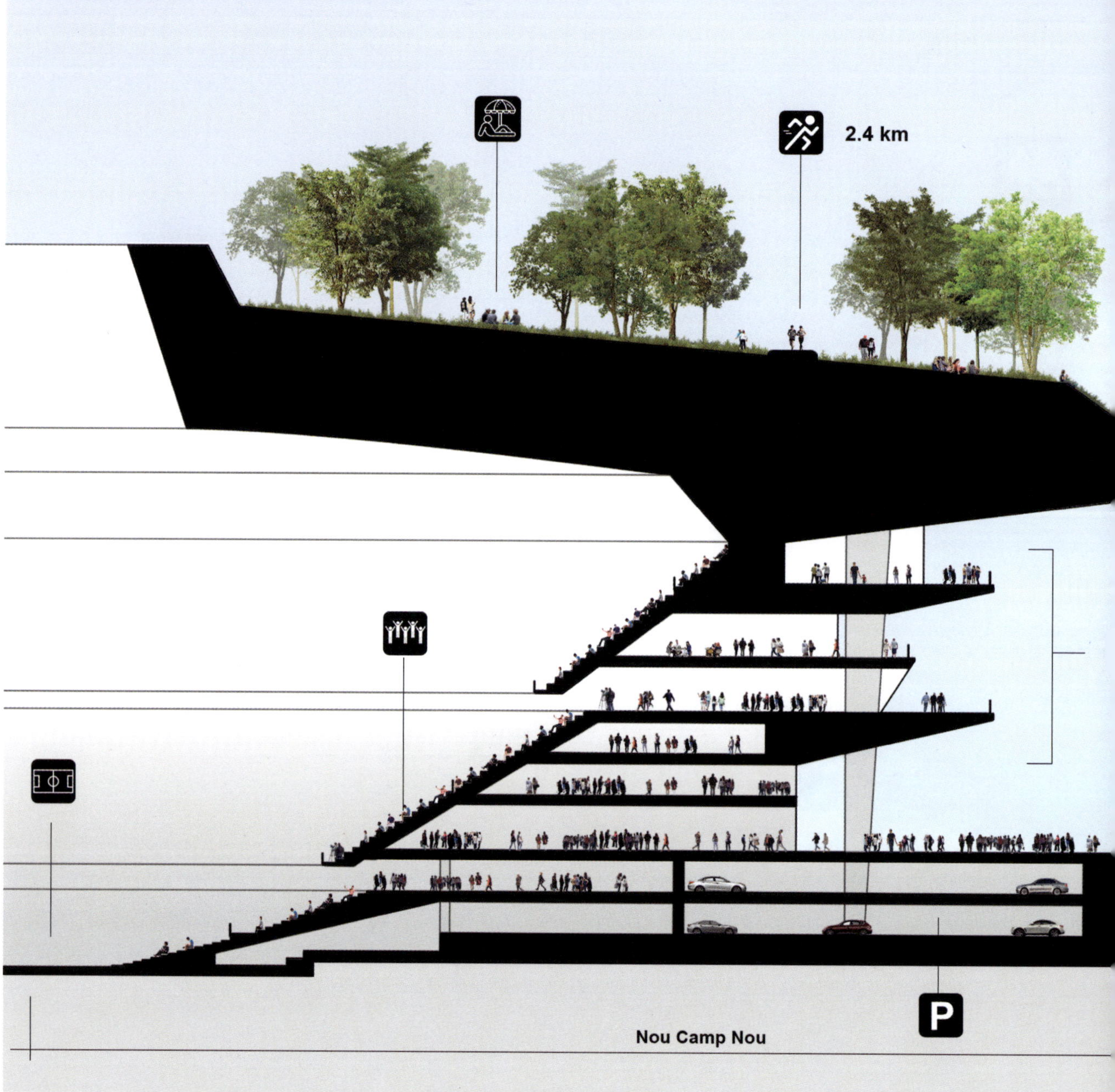

Renaturation
Bioarchitecture
Public Space
Recoversion
H
Av. Joan XXIII
Green space
Les Corts
Cemetery

NOU CAMP NOU

This project would help to create a new permeability that would allow the connection between the two neighborhoods of Les Corts and the University Area.

URBAN OASIS
ALGERIA

Hotel and office complex in Algeria. Green areas at ground-floor level and to the sides of the buildings improve air quality and comfort for end users of this complex. The buildings' curves allow air to circulate freely, a very important characteristic for this very warm climate.

The first two floors are dedicated to commercial premises and connect with the three towers that converge in a planted courtyard that improves natural ventilation.

Another strategic design feature is the importance given to balconies on all floors: this not only allows natural light to filter into the interior but also gives users constant contact with outdoor space. Another major advantage is gained in natural ventilation, reducing energy consumption and allowing the air inside to be renewed more frequently.

The nursery on the third floor is strategically located to allow children access to outdoor green spaces for socializing and activities. Finally, the office space is distributed over two towers interspersed with plants and expansive views.

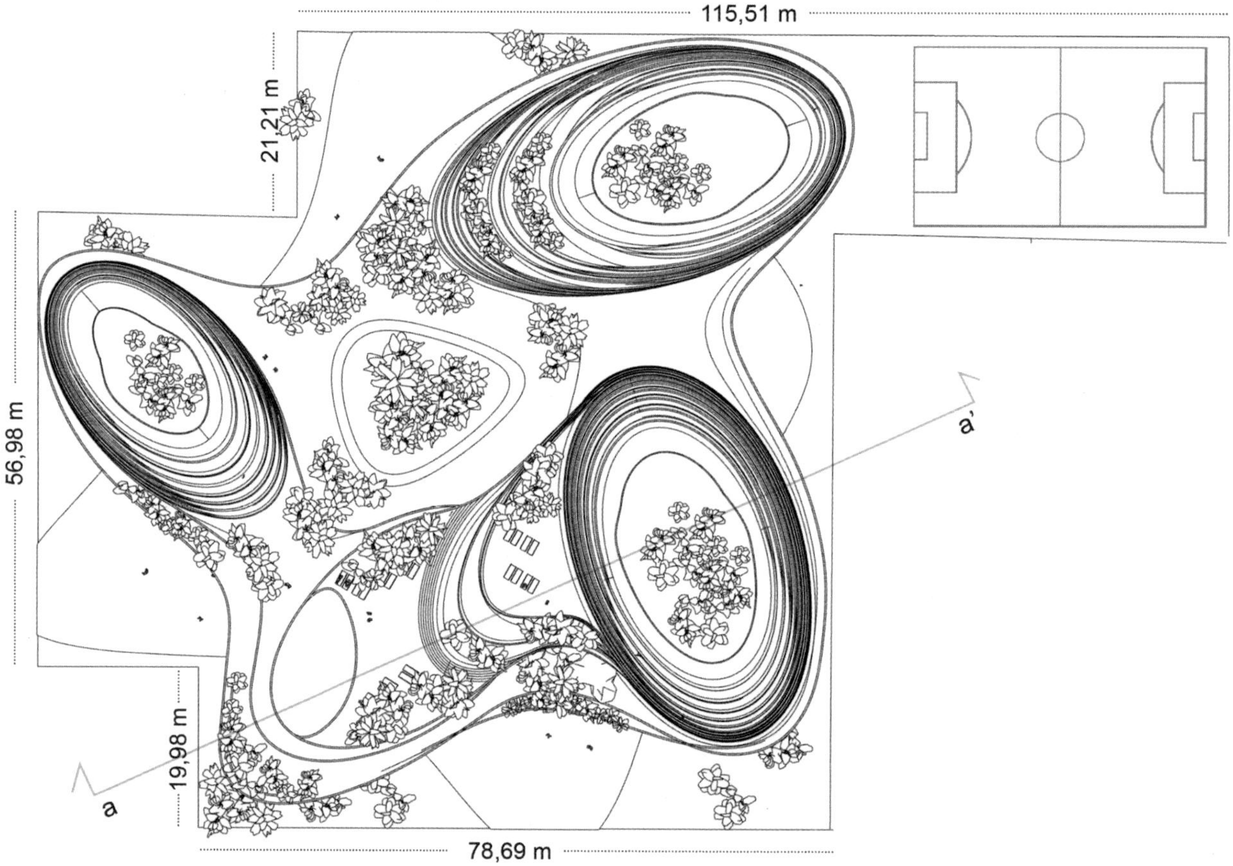
115,51 m
21,21 m
56,98 m
a'
a
19,98 m
78,69 m

Greenery
Natural Ventilation
Energy Efficency

The predominance of balconies in all floors, which not only filter the direct sunlight towards the inside, but also allows the user to have a constant contact with the outdoor space and benefit from natural ventilation, reducing energy consumption and allowing the inner air to be renovated more often.

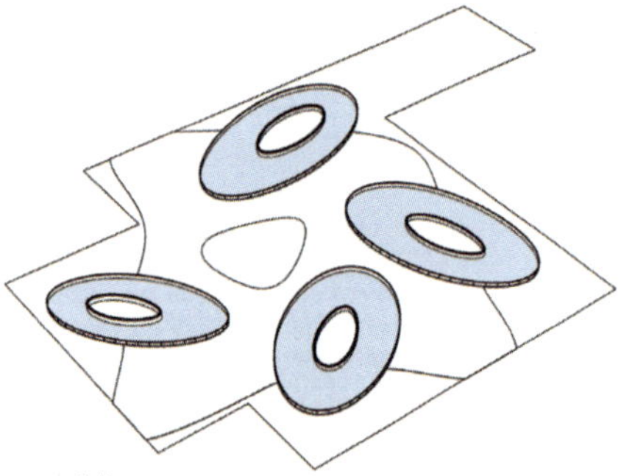

ground floor

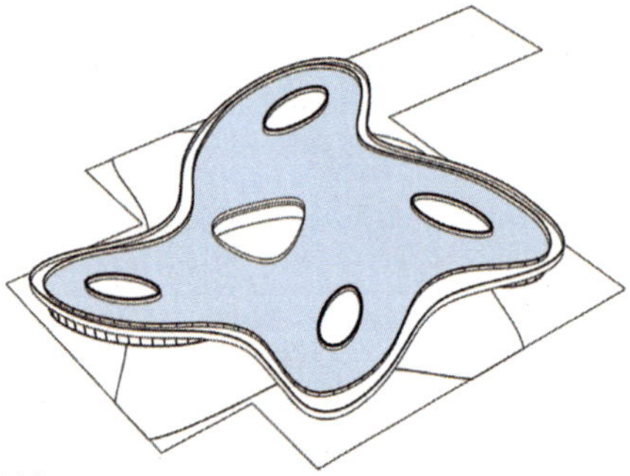

1st floor

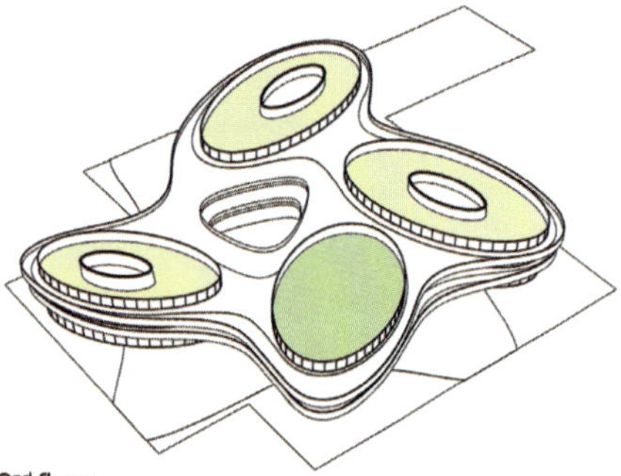

2nd floor

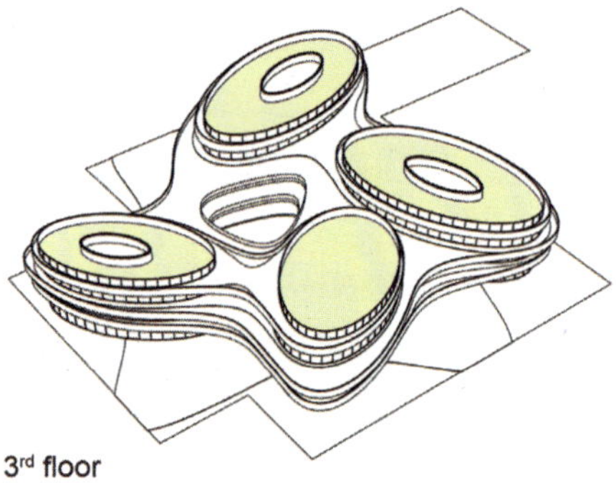

3rd floor

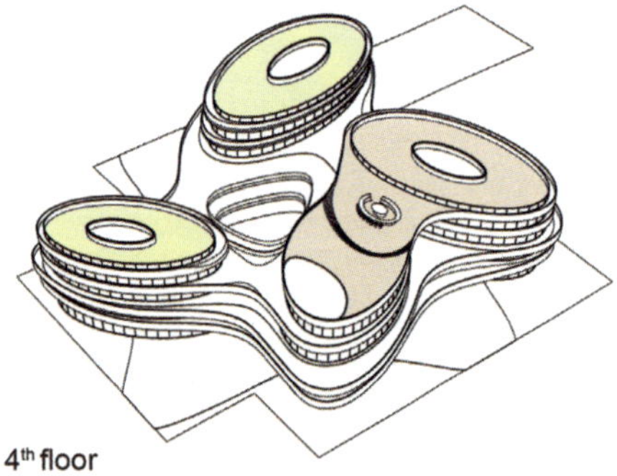

4th floor

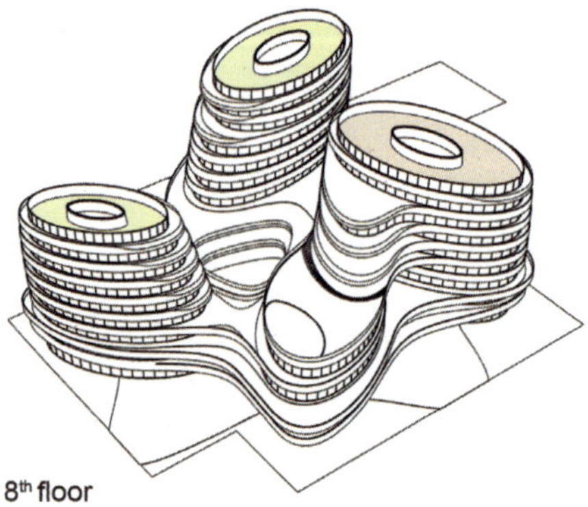

8th floor

office	18,427 m²		
hotel	10,786 m²		
retail	8,705 m²		
nursery	811 m²		
TOTAL	**38,729 m²**	**green area**	4008 m²

Urban Oasis is a mixed-use, with the hotel rooms and several facilities such as outdoor pool and garden, spa, gym, restaurant, two bars; the office space, split in two towers with intercalated greenery and generous views; and the nursery on the 3rd floor, strategically located so the children can have exterior green space for activities and gatherings.

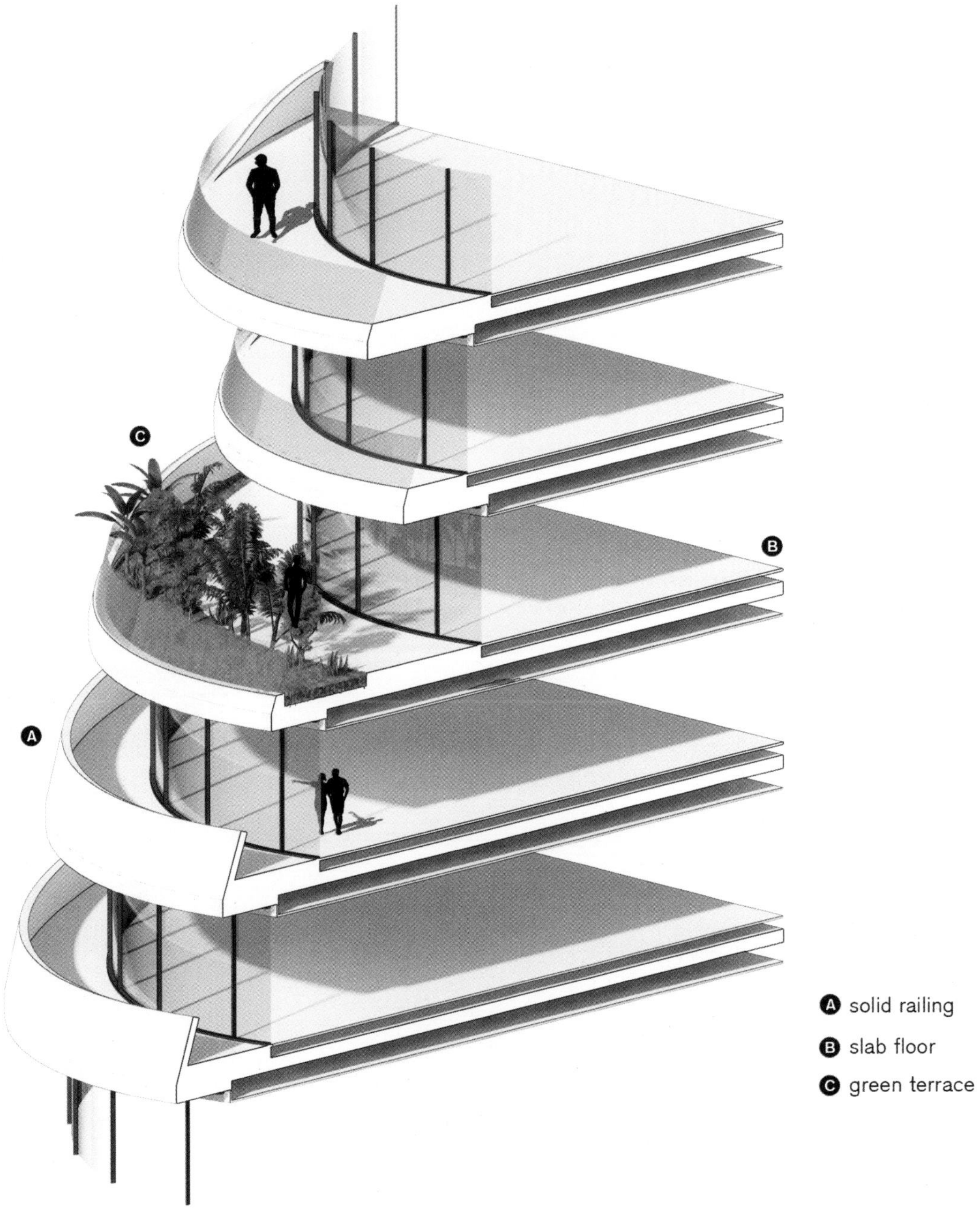

Green areas are found not only on the ground floor but in the vertical extension of the buildings as well, improving the air quality and comfort for the users.

KALMAR FLOODABLE CITY
SWEDEN

The Kalmar City Council (Sweden) proposed a new urban area with more than 3,000 homes in a well-known picturesque coastal area. The location is adjacent to an existing development of single-family homes. Given these parameters, the intervention is designed based on economic, social, environmental, and cultural sustainability through an urban development rooted in preserving the existing surroundings and reducing the territorial impact.

The proposal incorporates a statistical factor, since if the urban growth perpetuated the existing structure of single-family homes, it would occupy nearly 27% of the territory. Instead, the proposal incorporates a system of multi-family dwellings grouped into four-story towers. The towers concentrate eight standard dwellings each, and thus the territorial occupation is reduced to only 2%.

Following this reflection, the restructuring is intended to consolidate and protect existing landscapes by reusing roads as axes of articulation to manage the parallel realities of the countryside and the city. However, the predictions for flooding in the coming years show considerable increases over time.

That makes it necessary to account for elevating both the access roads and the multi-family units on the ground floors by a margin of approximately three meters. This measure serves to complement the overall framework with a parameter that is no less important, and which encompasses all the others listed so far: the project's long-term viability.

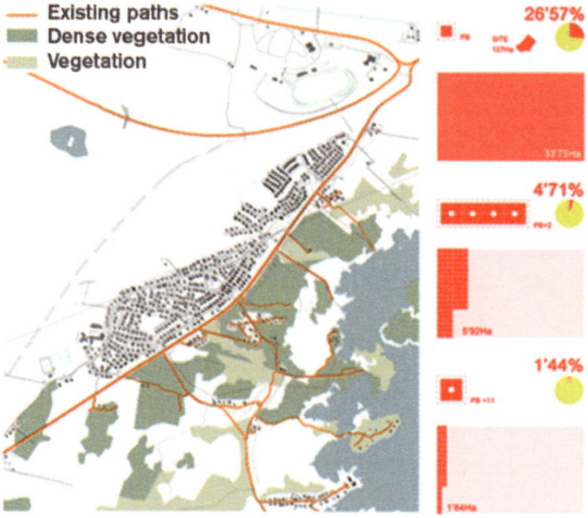

Restructuring is intended to consolidate and protect existing landscapes by reusing roads as articulating axes in the face of the parallel realities between the countryside and the city.

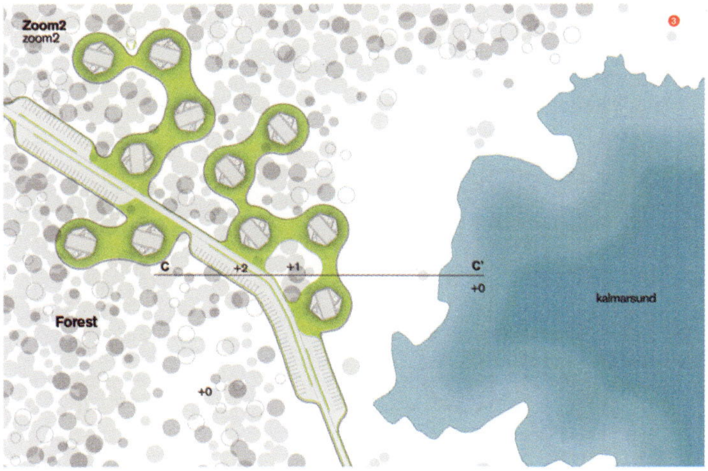

C-C' Section

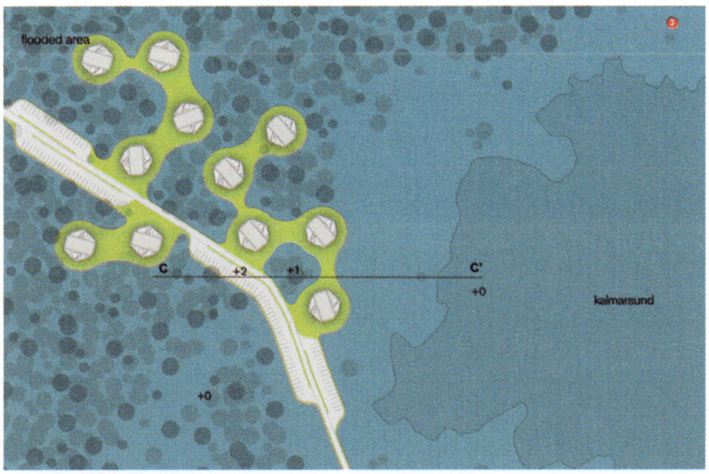

C-C' section

Project's aim was the conservation of the areas of high environmental value that constitute the identity of Kalmar.

The flood forecast in the coming years increases considerably over time, which makes it necessary to anticipate the elevation on the ground to an approximate margin of three meters.

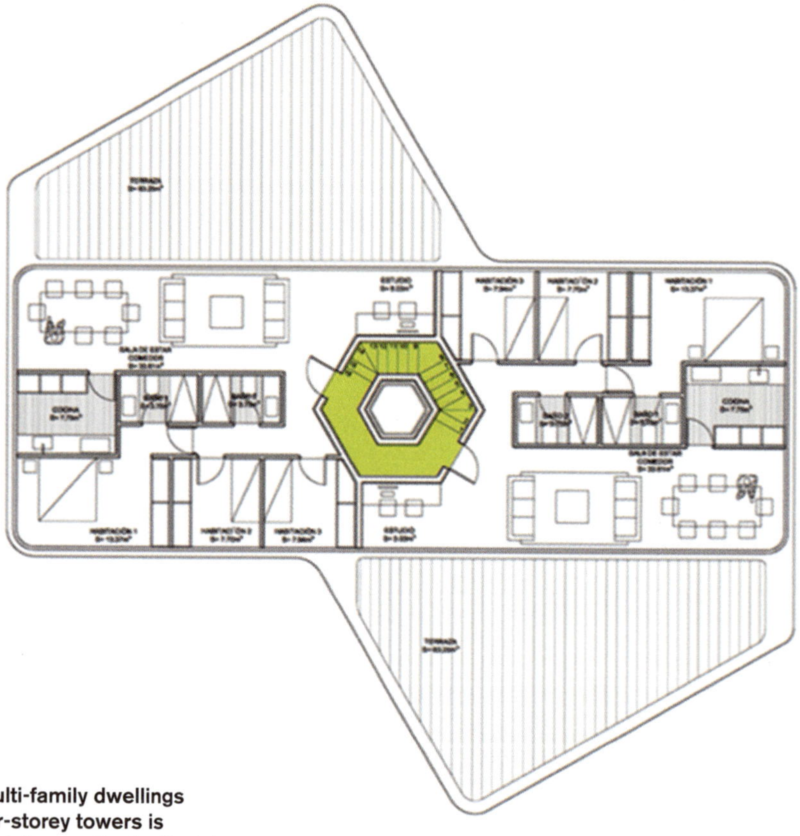

A system of multi-family dwellings grouped in four-storey towers is proposed, and doing so, the territorial occupation would be reduced to only 2% instead of 27%.

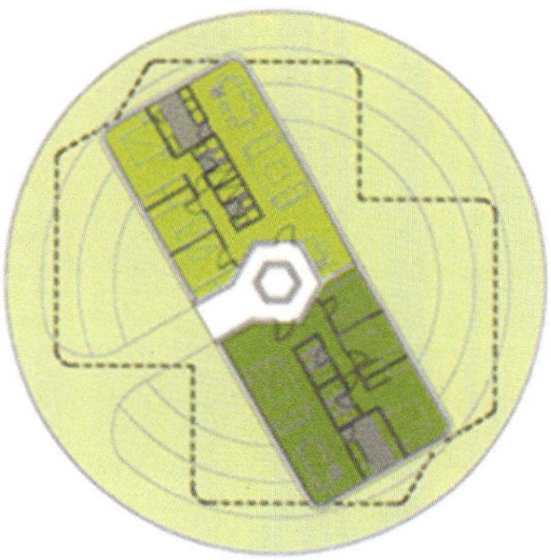

P1

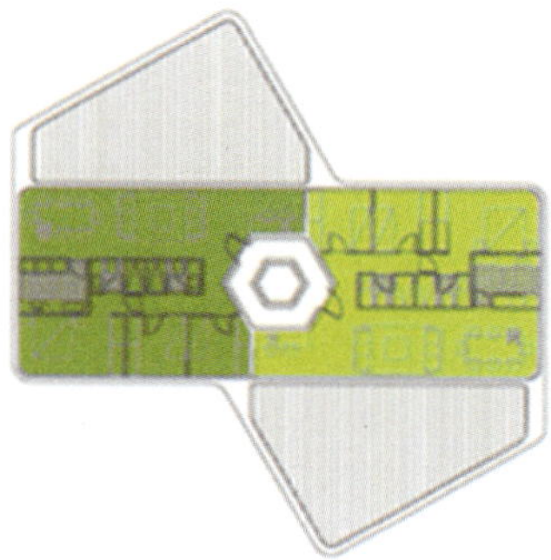

P2

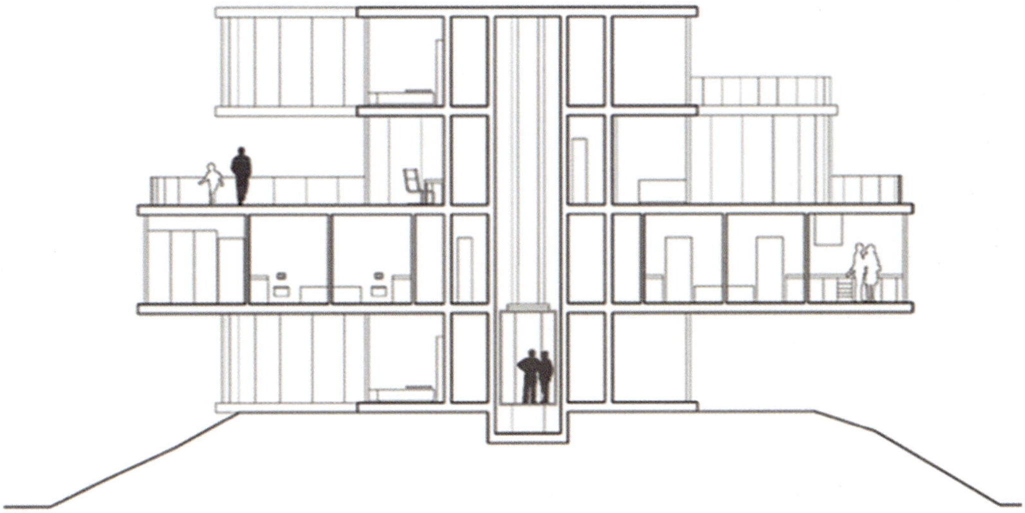

Low Impact
Conservation
Viability

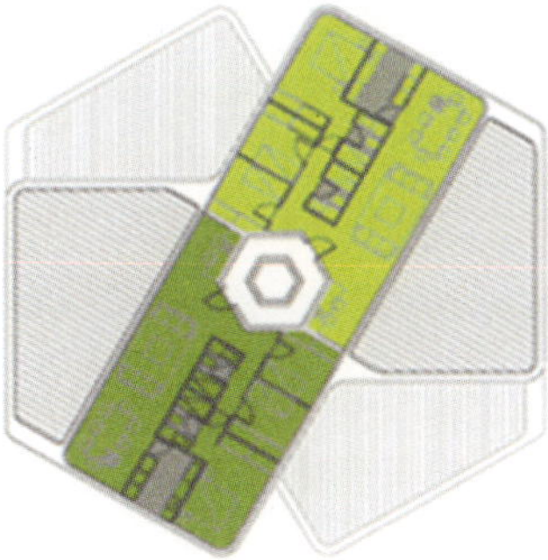

P3

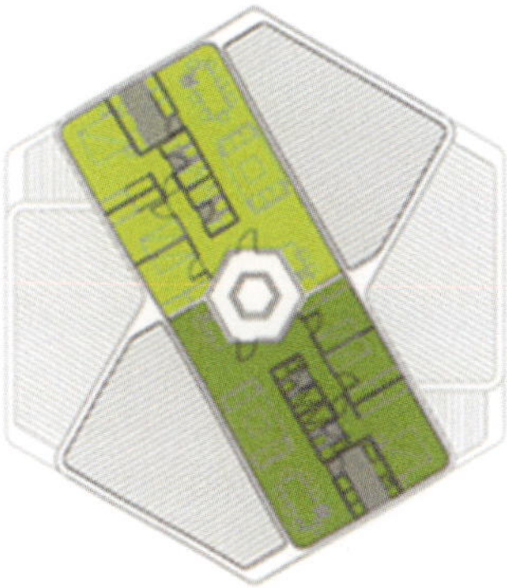

P4

The intervention was based on an economic, social, environmental and cultural sustainability.

ON-A's designs work as a catalyst for the creation of positive emotions among their inhabitants; physical/ visual well-being and comfort contribute to the occupants' health and the flexible usability of the designed spaces.

Emotion
Lifestyle
&
Inhabiting

RICARDO One of the meanings of ON-A is the combination of "emotion" and "architecture", but another is "innovation" and "architecture". How do you combine the two concepts (emotion and innovation) in your projects? What kind of emotions do you want to elicit in the inhabitants or the people who see your buildings?

JORDI We try to design buildings that convey something, beyond just resolving a program. In the Lounge Bar, which is called "5 Senses", the client's original idea was to awaken the senses. That's why we worked with lights, atmospheres, even smells. The goal was to bring out totally different emotions based on theme nights. Based on that, we understand emotion as the creation of singular, special spaces that evoke feelings. Innovating in program, materials and spaces is an undercurrent in our architecture.

EDUARDO We did something similar with Sant Pau Cultural Center. We needed to cover the cloisters to protect the existing chapel, so we created a new space using a new way of handling light. Up to that point, the cloister was only lit by daylight. We tried to conjure the vision of being inside a Gothic cathedral, using the openings of a honeycomb geometry, like a huge stained-glass window with ETFE membranes, like large domes inspired by cathedrals. That's how we resolved the program while also adding emotion to the space.

RICARDO Another thing that is very present in your architecture is the use of color. At what point in your designs do you introduce it? What other architectural strategies do you use to generate emotional effects in spaces?

JORDI Everything comes from the commission itself. In the 5 Sentidos Lounge Bar, we had to create different environments: from being in a jungle to a glacial atmosphere. In the case of the Cricursa stand, the colors coincide with the corporate image. In Sant Pau Cultural Center, we used white cones so they would accurately reflect the warmth of natural light. For the Drassanes Metro Station, the colors and the use of light were dictated by the program. Initially, the station was all dark and black. Its users are often tourists, and there were problems with theft and people falling on the platforms due to poor lighting. Those problems were solved by the new configuration, the light colors, the red from the TMB brand in the connecting tunnels, and the right lighting. The façade of the Valdaya Wineries uses shades that are reminiscent of the color of wine. In fact, we suggested pieces that would recall a bunch of grapes, with reddish and burgundy tones. The pavement was made of hexagonal pieces in varied green tones, imitating a vineyard. Each design has its own history, but we always try to look for the emotions that it can evoke.

Drassanes Metro Station, Barcelona.

RICCARDO When you're working with domestic programs, both single-family and multi-family homes, what type of inhabitant do you have in mind when you're designing those spaces?

EDUARDO For a single family it's like designing a tailored suit. We research what the client wants, although we sometimes suggest changes. As for multi-family buildings, if it isn't a public competition for the administration, we have to stick with what the developer wants, in terms of distributions and so on, because it's a very traditional sector. We don't entirely believe in the housing typologies being offered today: living-dining room, kitchen and bedrooms, even when it might be for a couple who doesn't want children or who may have them later in life.

We've designed housing with typologies that are more "open plan" and adaptable, depending on each family's needs.

RICARDO In both single-family and multi-family houses, the exterior-interior relationship is always given an intense focus, and exterior spaces are increasingly important, with the addition of terraces and balconies.

JORDI We're currently developing quite a few multi-family homes, with very commercial concepts. But we're also involved in lots of research projects where we investigate different forms of dwelling. Take, for example, a detached house we designed in Gavà – the Black Jenga House – located on the seafront.

The client had a very conventional idea of the living-dining room and garden on the ground floor, the children's bedrooms on the first floor, and the master bedroom on the second floor.

We turned it around, because you only get the sea views from the first floor. So, we asked them, where do you spend the most time? And it turns out that 80% of their waking hours are spent in the living room, the kitchen, and the dining room. So, we told them that was where they should have the views, and we moved the public program to the first floor. That's why the terraces are raised, with views of the sea, with sun in the morning or the afternoon. Then the children's bedrooms were on the ground floor, freeing up space for a large pool. On the first floor we put in a jacuzzi. And upstairs, the master bedroom has views towards the sea, a giant dressing room, a home cinema, and a spa. The result was a totally different house than what they had imagined.

We've done other studies, like the house with a green roof, where, with one simple gesture, we generated a house that is entirely opaque towards the street and entirely open towards the yard. Or the Loop House, a study of a continuous dwelling, where the ground floor leads up to the first floor, and the terrace connects with the roof. In that case, the program was centered around a courtyard, creating transition areas with stair seating for small events.

Black Jenga House, Gavà. Three distinct masses that, depending on their aspect, generate and protect a set of terraces.

A system of fragmented folds governs the formal strategy of this project to achieve a unique appearance enriched by a particularly evocative geometry.

Black Jenga House, Gavà.

Another multi-family project is the Windmill Towers, a residential complex in a forest, with a limited footprint or impact. To that end, we created an underground parking lot which provides the connections to the central cores of the buildings. The unique characteristic of the complex is that we generated duplexes, and the rotation of the different stories provides a lot of height between one terrace and the next. That gives you very large, sunny terraces and the feeling of a multi-story house in a forested setting.
And then, instead of taking up space for the common areas around the pool, we put them on the roof. That way you just have the footprints of the towers and the small path that connects them.

We also participated in a Europan Competition in Kalmar, Sweden. The theme was planning urban growth in an area that is frequently flooded, and which will be flooded in the future due to sea level rise. We took advantage of the existing roads to preserve the vegetation on the site as much as possible. We elevated the roads and created residential towers connected to those roads, like cells growing around them. We used a distribution that, ultimately, is similar to the Windmill Towers: a central core, two units per story, large sunny terraces, with multiple orientations and all of them with views. If water levels were to rise, the roads, the parking areas, and the dwellings would be protected.

In the case of another residential building in Empuriabrava —Pattern Building—, the developer wanted a conventional typology, but we proposed incorporating duplexes, because it freed up space to create patios, gardens and an indoor pool, with a more community-centered concept. The entire complex was covered with an envelope to generate privacy for the more private spaces.

The rotation of the different stories gives you very large, sunny terraces and the feeling of a multi-story house in a forested setting.

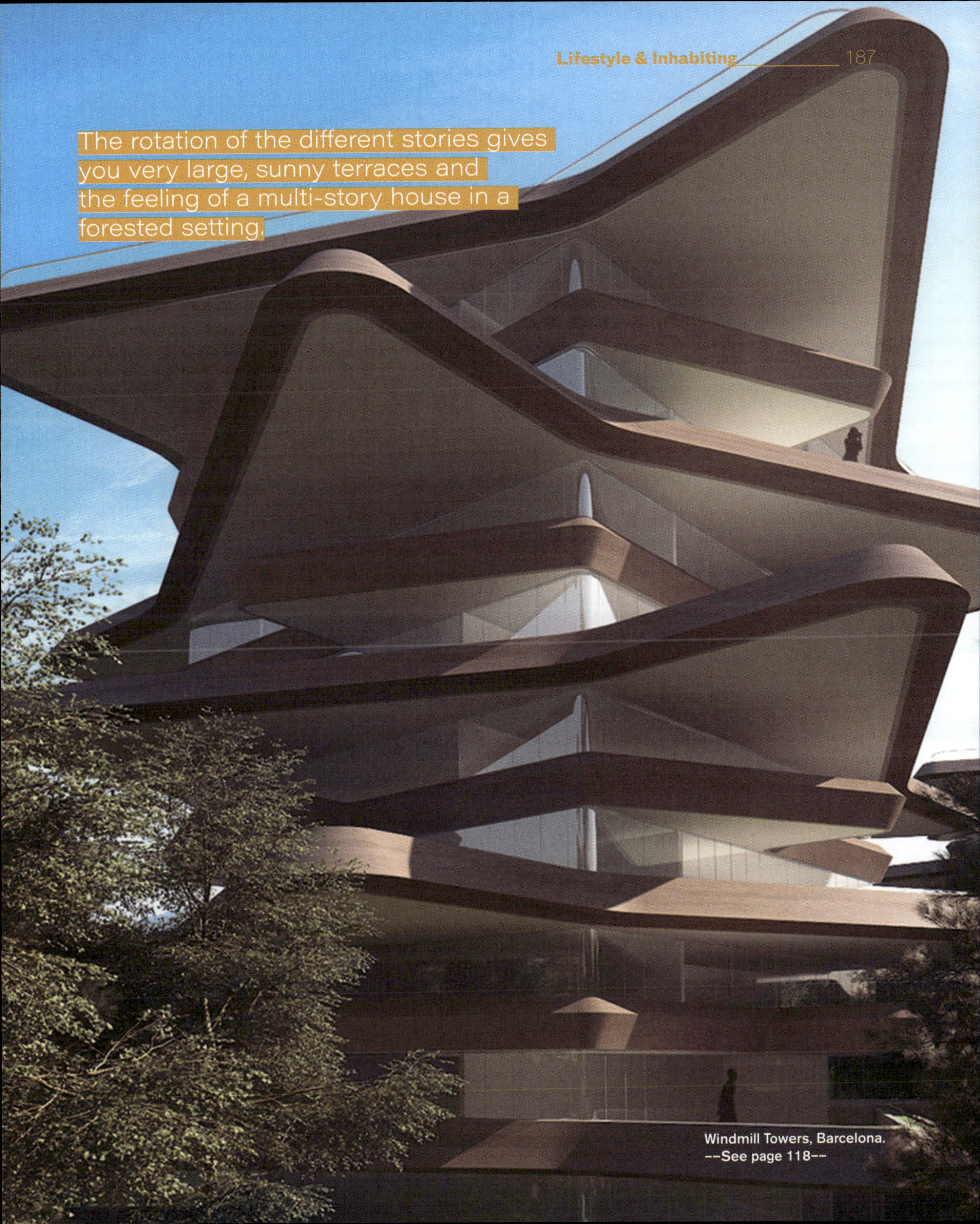

Windmill Towers, Barcelona.
--See page 118--

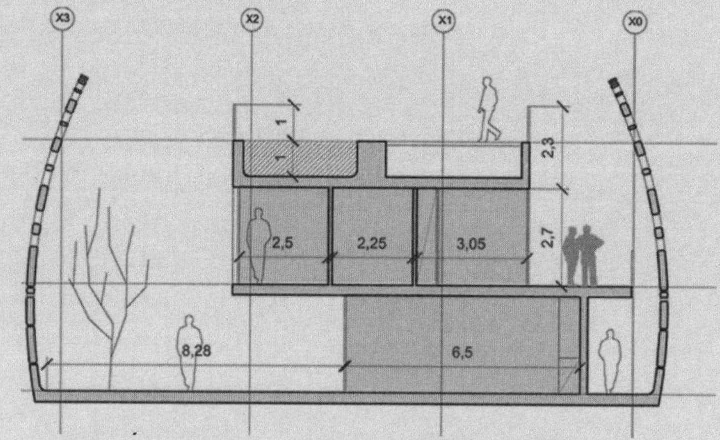

Pattern Building, Empuriabrava. **--See page 206--**

RICARDO How do you go about achieving emotion and innovation in programs associated with leisure or temporary occupation, like hotels?

JORDI Hotels are defined by the program and the style the client wants. For example, the Classic Hotel project was a renovation of the Palace in Barcelona, and we offered a reinterpretation of the classic decor. We developed a play of wallpapers, with print patterns, taking a detail from the fabric and scaling it to use as a motif in the hotel room.

The Urban Hotel in Almería was intended for conferences, so it has a more technological facet, with screens to be used for events. We gave it warmth through interior spaces with much more functional lines, designed for a workspace.

We did another hotel in Benidorm, more leisure-oriented, where the common areas like the roof were the most important elements. We imagined it white, with much more light, because it's in the Mediterranean, and we played with the warm tones of the wood.

Classic Hotel, Barcelona. Spacious and comfortable rooms designed in keeping with the latest technology and decorative Renaissance-inspired motifs and patterns.

EDUARDO The Blade is a hotel where we designed three oases within the building. Since it was in Riyadh, a city without green areas, we decided to put them inside the building itself. The open areas helped us avoid the wind effect of skyscrapers. The rooms were conventional, but the public uses associated with the hotel could vary.

RICARDO How do you approach innovation in more common programs, like offices or workspaces?

JORDI For the National Water Company Tower, a corporate tower in Riyadh, we invoked fluidity, the geometries generating the rivers and meanders on the façade. We wanted to create a different feeling with the play of light at night on the façades, reminiscent of the flow of water. We created an upward spiral effect by rotating a square floor plan around a single central axis, so that you get more office space the higher you go.

We developed a play of wallpapers, with print patterns, taking a detail from the fabric and scaling it to use as a motif in the hotel room.

Classic Hotel, Barcelona.

This hotel offers unique, spacious and comfortable rooms designed in keeping with the latest technology in terms of their features and characteristics.

Urban Hotel, Almería.

Boutique Hotel, Barcelona.

1. Wet zone
2. Storage
3. Screen tv - desk

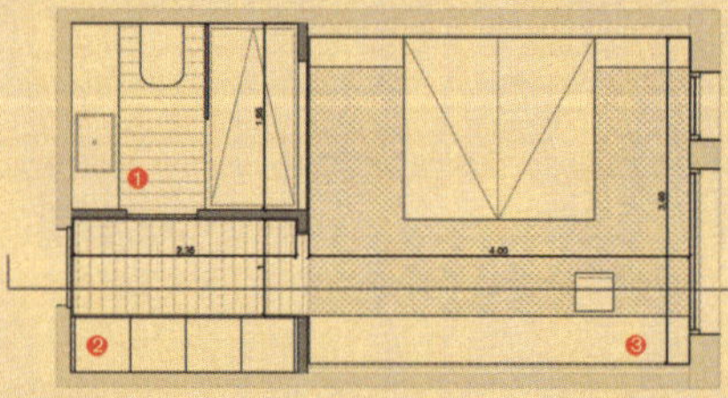

Room Floor Type

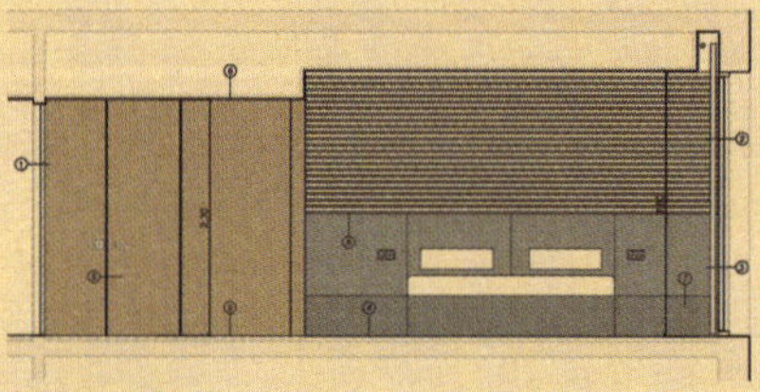

Section Room Type

Section Room Type

1. Oiled oak wood paneling. Installation by screwing to the secondary profiles with distance between axes
2. Oak wood profile grid 200 mm wide and 22 mm thick with alternating half-wood joints
3. 7mm thick lacquered DM board
4. 3mm thick pearl gray carpet
5. 22 mm thick natural maple wood parquet
6. False ceiling plasterboard to shelt climatization
7. Bedside tables in lacquered wood anchored to the wall
8. Led lighting
9. Smooth oiled oak wood door

0 0,5 1

The interior has a style and character all its own that exudes exclusivity and offers a welcoming atmosphere perfect for guests on business trips.

Urban Hotel, Almería.

That's how we created a unique, more expressive building. From certain perspectives you get these surprising shapes, and from others it looks like a rectangular volume, since the diagonal of the lower square is the same as the side of the square above it. As for the functional distribution, we aimed for a maximum open area, since we had the structure along the façade and then a central core.

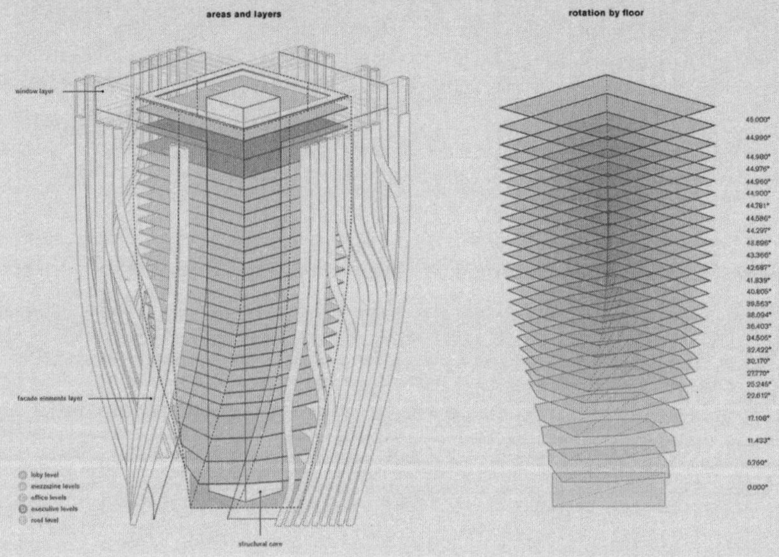

National Water Company Tower, Riyadh. The volume is twisted to define a wave-like profile as well as the façade, making reference to the forms of moving water.
--See page 52--

RICARDO You also try to create these emotions in public spaces and parks where you've designed a series of interconnected uses that offer a different kind of experience. Do you use the same strategy as with closed spaces?

JORDI For the Llano Amarillo park in Algeciras, ON-A's first competition, we were dealing with a series of large closed public programs, including a congress hall, but also an open-air auditorium, areas for the rowing club, restaurants, and open-air parking. The green topography that housed those open uses was the foundation for the entire project. A blanket of green was laid out over a huge space, creating hills and valleys that generated microclimates for each of the programs. We played with the topography and the vegetation depending on its distance from the sea. We also did an in-depth study of the trees in keeping with the program, working with native species, aiming for low water consumption and easy maintenance.

EDUARDO As for the "lifestyle" of these parks, which normally occupy a single level, the difference with Llano Amarillo was the idea of generating open areas in the depressions, where we situated the program of play areas, sports courts or public squares. The elevated areas, in contrast, were reserved for the architectural program, i.e., the buildings. That gave us a different way of perceiving the spaces. You could be next to a restaurant, but you didn't realize it was a building because you were in a depression, in a play area, and what you saw next to you was a mountain, not a building.

Llano Amarillo Park, Algeciras.
-- See Page 90--

Landscaped pathways, sports circuits and cycling paths are the foundation of the initiative to transform a strategic enclave of the city into an exceptional spot for recreation.

Llano Amarillo Park, Algeciras.

JORDI Another similar competition was for the Taichung Gateway Park, located in the area of the old airport, which intended to generate a series of neighborhoods and districts that were articulated by the park. Our solution was similar to the Llano Amarillo. We brought the green over the streets and dropped the streets into tunnels, creating continuity for the park. We also generated lakes aimed to take advantage of the water in the area and clean it. The other programs, including a tower, a city of film, and other facilities, were arranged amid those organic volumes.

EDUARDO Another urban space that we designed was the pergola for Plaça de les Glòries in Barcelona, a temporary shade space in the park where several pedestrian traffic flows converged. We proposed a programmatic topography to create shade, but we housed the program in boxes: some contained lighting, others contained plants or acted as bleachers. They were cubes made from OSB panels, which could increase or decrease in volume depending on our interest.

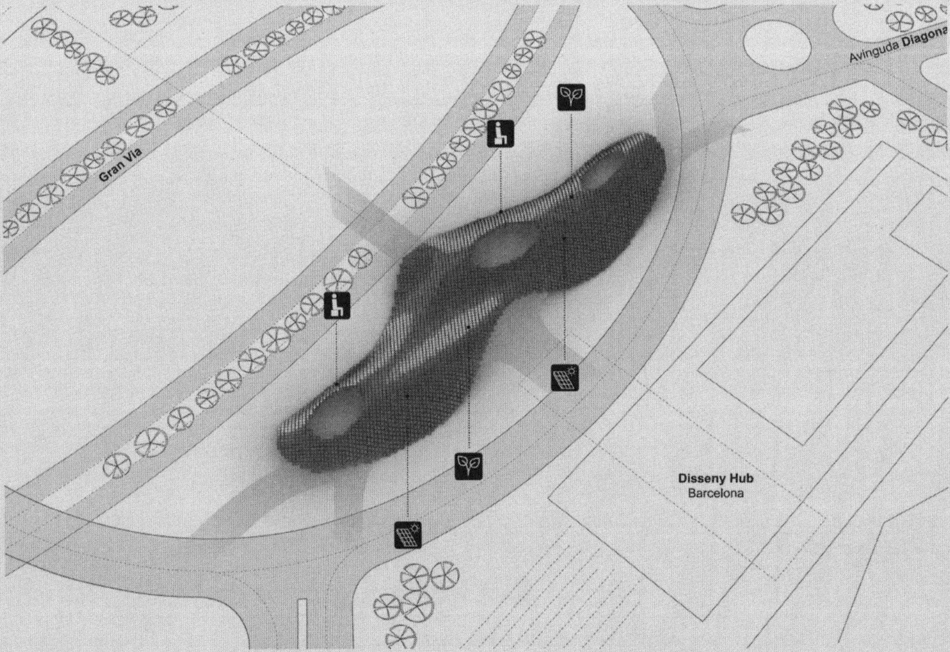

The Green Shadow, Barcelona.

The Green Shadow, Barcelona.

A pergola that offers sun protection and blocks views of traffic while serving as a landmark for pedestrians, enhancing the public space and capturing solar energy.

The Green Shadow, Barcelona.

RICARDO Finally, what ideas have you developed that involve building a city ex novo? How have you applied the innovations you've been talking about on an urban and territorial scale?

JORDI We did a project for a new city, called Neom, in Saudi Arabia, which was meant to be a technology city, a city of the future. We thought about what it would be like to live in a hostile environment, like the desert. We've always liked imagining how we might inhabit the Earth in a much more efficient way. Technology can give us the possibility of living in environments that would once have been uninhabitable, in a much more sustainable way while adapting to the extreme conditions.

Today, we can generate clean energy almost anywhere on the planet, using the sun, the wind, the tides, etc. We can travel at high speeds much more efficiently, using technologies like the hyperloop – small capsules for five people that can run at a speed of 1,000 km/h – or drones that make it possible to transport objects without having to generate infrastructure and consume territory. Increasingly, we can create buildings that consume less and recycle their own waste. We applied all this for a competition in the Arctic, the Hermetic City, a building that is a city in itself. For the competition, we had to propose a development for more than 1,000 people in the North Pole, which would be connected by a hyperloop.

Instead of designing horizontal growth, we proposed building a tower with a central core and attaching the houses to it like prefabricated capsules that could be added depending on the need. It would be a building that grows as the inhabitants arrive. The building envelope itself captures energy. At the base, we would centralize food production, waste management, water. We proposed a building that wouldn't generate any outside waste. It would be managed through the core and the base; there would be composting in an area with greenhouses and agriculture to produce part of the food for the tower's inhabitants. We also designed platforms where drones could land. The configuration of the tower was based on triangles so that all the houses would have optimum orientation.

In the post-COVID era, this efficient adaptation, which we looked at as an interesting idea a priori, now seems like a necessity.

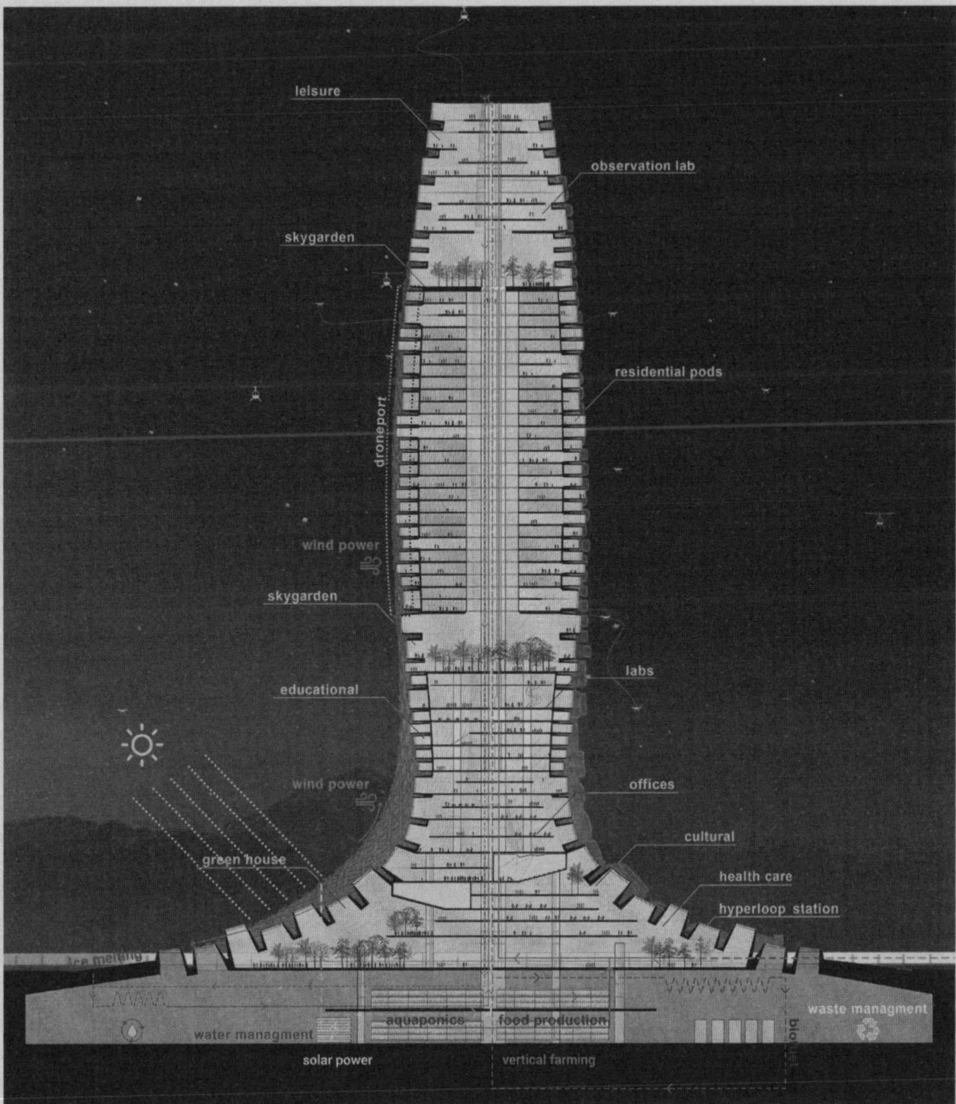

Hermeticity.
--See page 115--

PATTERN BUILDING
SPAIN

This design for an apartment building on one of the main channels of the Empuriabrava network of waterways is an example of the application of parametric architecture that promises to regenerate the identity of the sector through innovation and technology.

Located on one of the main streets in Empuriabrava is this unique apartment building design, the brainchild of ON-A. Taking into account its setting in a shopping area, the ground floor is planned to house commercial premises, a parking area in the basement and duplex apartments with gardens. Leisure and relaxation are catered for with solarium and pool area on the roof, offering stunning close-up views of the sea.

The exterior enclosing wall is the result of explorations in parametric architecture using key resources such as CAD/CAM digital production. Working from this basis, the concept includes a façade that functions as a visual filter, generating a harmonious overall image for the building with a continuous latticework wall rendered in glass fiber reinforced concrete. The design affords privacy to the building's apartments and gardens on the main façade, as well as giving the whole a cutting-edge architectural identity.

Located in a shopping area, the ground floor planned to house commercial premises.

The façade functions as a visual filter, generating a harmonious overall image for the building with a continuous latticework wall rendered in glass fiber reinforced concrete.

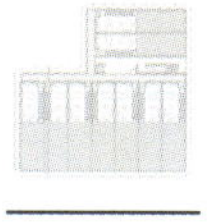

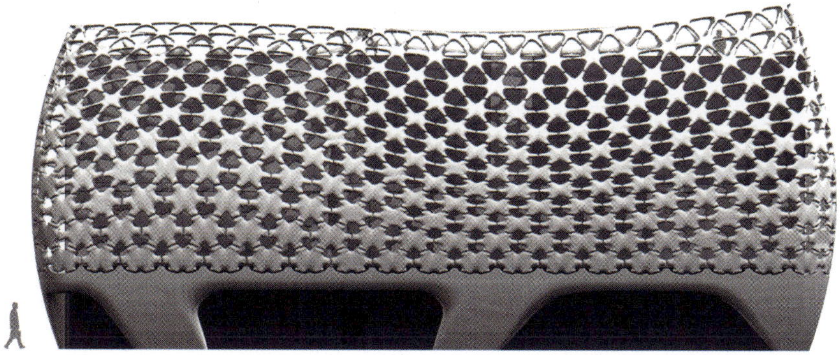

Greenery Latticework Parametric

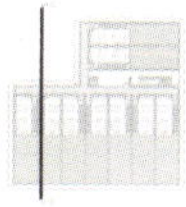

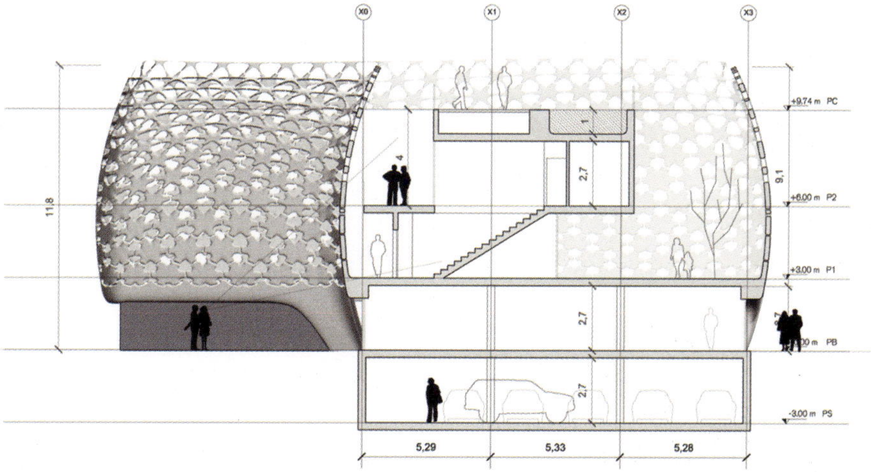

The exterior enclosing wall explores parametric design.

COSMETIC SHOP
COSMETIC
COSMETIC

Leisure and relaxation are catered for with solarium and pool area on the roof, offering stunning close-up views of the sea.

The latticework wall affords privacy to the building's apartments and gardens on the main façade.

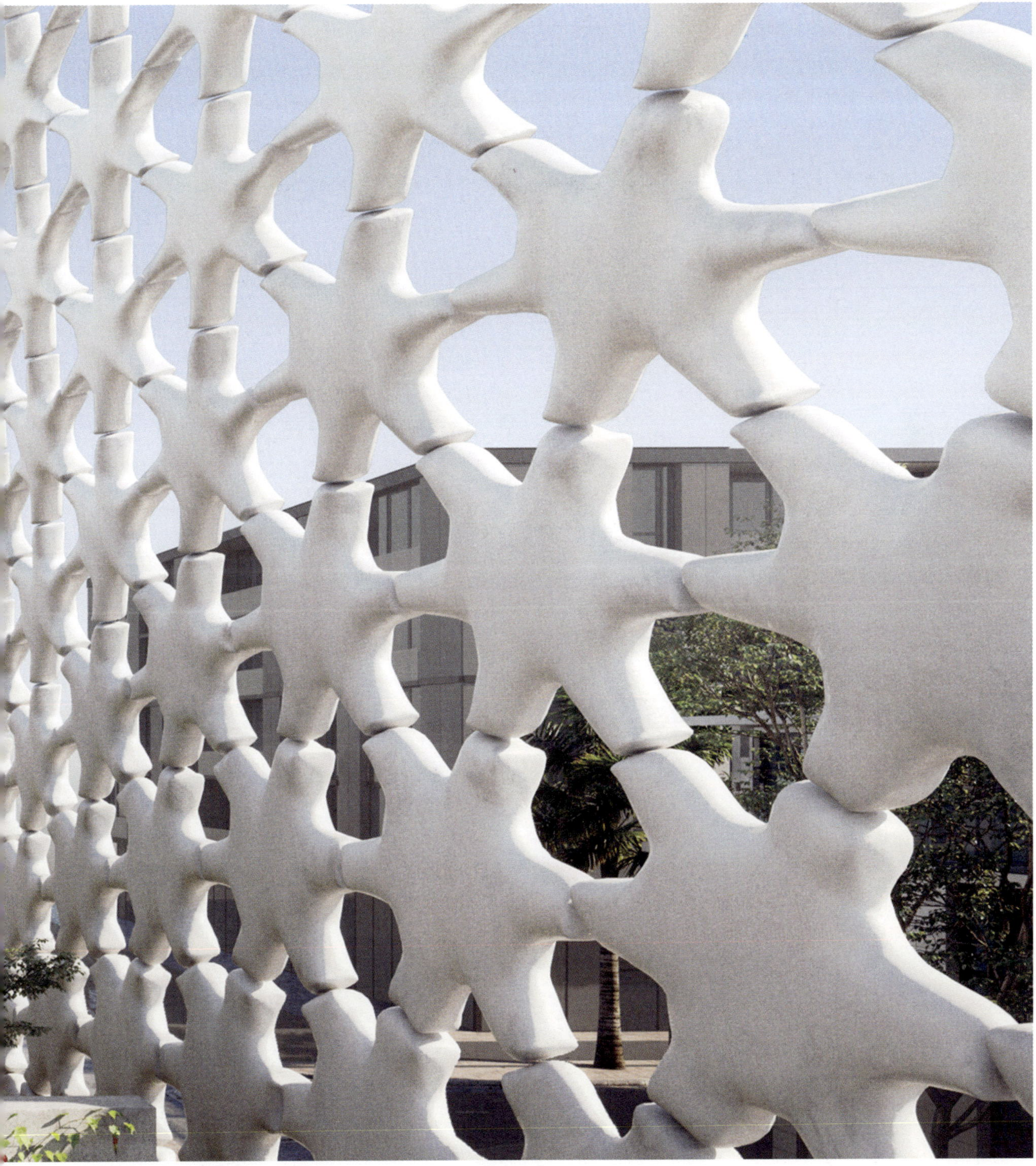

HOTEL AND SPA BENIDORM

SPAIN

Located on a picturesque site near the beach in Benidorm, sitting atop a mountain with sweeping views of the sea and the city, this large five-star Spa and Hotel complex is characterized by its unique architecture.

Recreational and leisure activities are arranged on a large podium with multiple terraces that house pools, a restaurant, spa and an events area. This guarantees that these common areas and the rooms on the upper floors all have exceptional views and an excellent orientation.

The common areas are thus concentrated on the lower floors, and a 40-story tower houses the 450 rooms, topped with a sky-bar on the last floor. Outside the sky-bar is an infinity pool on a large terrace with sun loungers, offering the best views of the complex, which is designed to function year-round for events and congresses and for visits to the spa with its hydrotherapy area.

All rooms have sea views and are accessed via a corridor along the back façade. Inside, materials such as light-colored wood are used to generate warmth and brightness.

H10
BENIDORM

Well-being Terrace Uniqueness

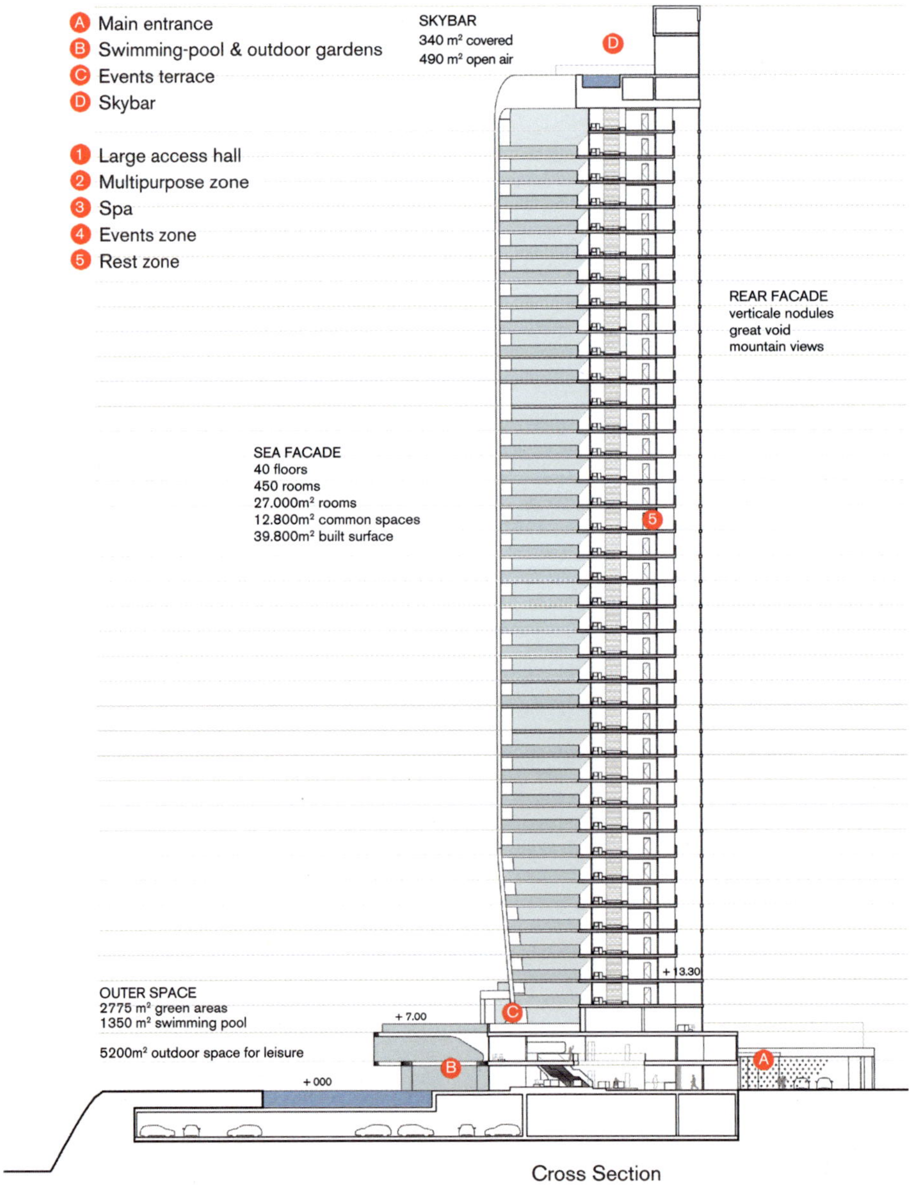

Cross Section

Recreational and leisure activities are arranged on a large podium with multiple terraces that house pools, a restaurant, spa and an events area.

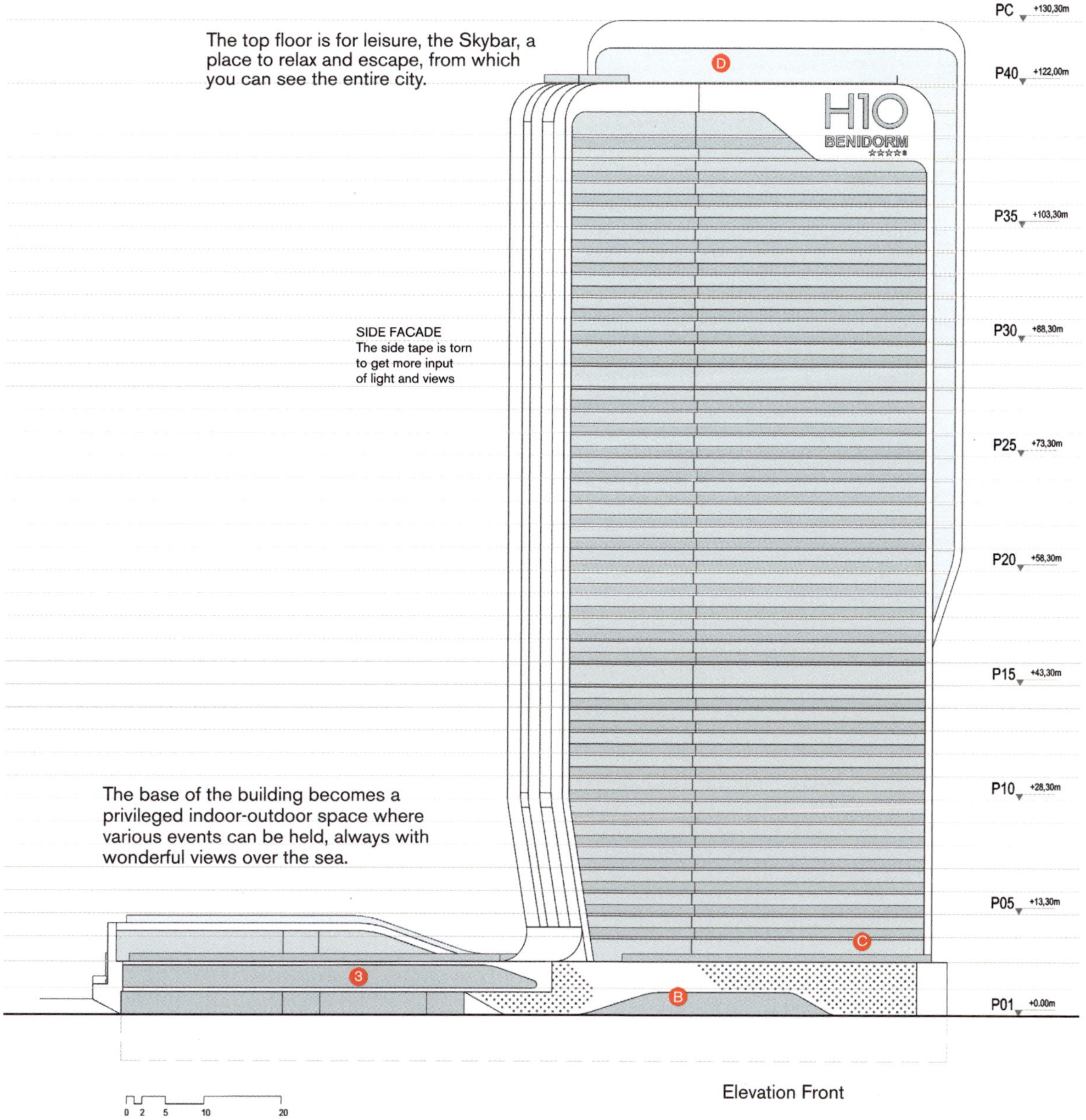

Elevation Front

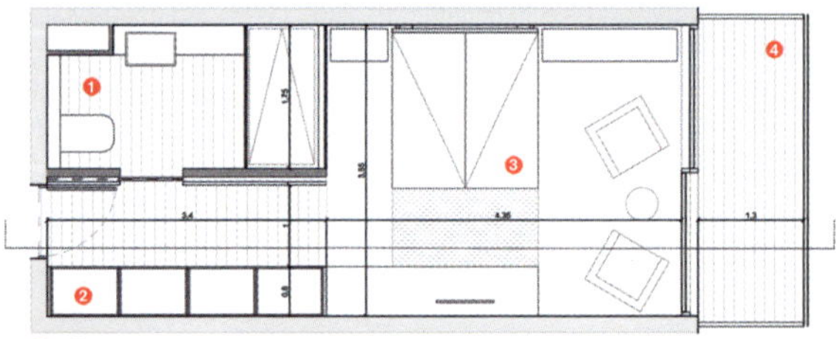

Floor type room

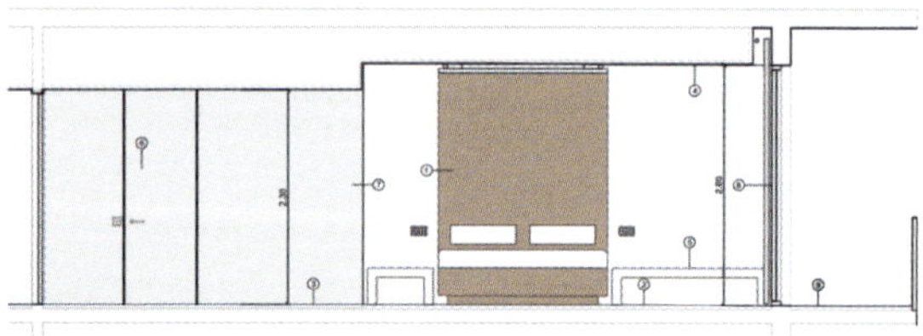

Section type room

1. wet areas
2. storage
3. bedroom
4. terrace

① Structure in oiled oak wood, screwed to the secondary profiles and side led lighting
② 3 mm thick pearl gray carpet
③ 22 mm thick natural maple wood parquet
④ False ceiling plasterboard to allow installations and air conditioning
⑤ Bedside tables of lacquered wood ral 2010 color
⑥ Sliding door in 40 mm lacquered wood, 9010 ral 9010 color
⑦ Plasterboard partition wall ral 9010 color
⑧ Aluminium sliding door
⑨ Exterior wooden platform on battens

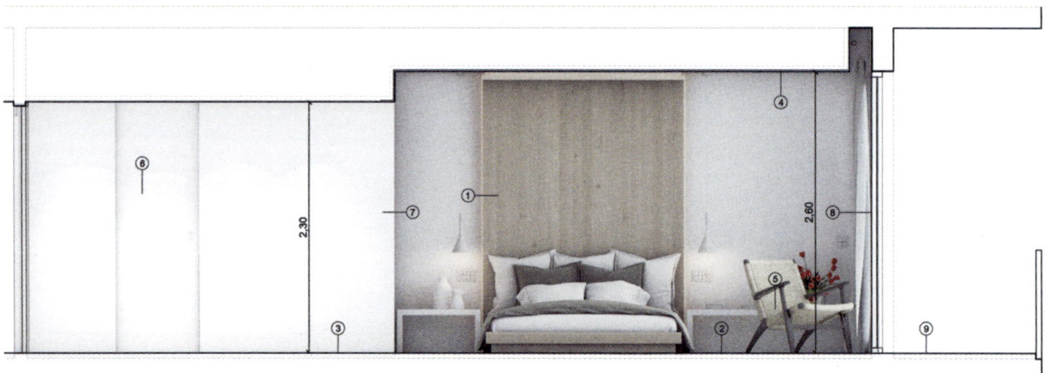

Section type room

0 0,5 1

H10
BENIDORM
SPA

H10
BENIDORM
SKYBAR

ZENIT TOWER
ANDORRA

This residential tower is a 1,828 m^2 plot at the center of Andorra la Vella. Designed to combine various uses and in keeping with the regulations specific to this Pyrenean valley, the built volumes must respect the maximum floor area ratio.

The design makes it possible to adjust the project for maximum buildable area. A reduction in the size of the ground floor and first floor ensures compliance with the 15% easement for right of way, creating an interior passageway that supports circulations and tertiary uses at the street level.

The volume is emptied out on the following floors (2 through 10) to reduce the total floor area. The maximum possible occupation is maintained on the following floors (11 through 15). The final floors (16 to 20) are concentrated in one of the volumes, taking advantage of a total of 274 m per floor.
It also incorporates two elevator cores to facilitate vertical circulation. As for the envelope, visual relationships with the exterior are enhanced by arranging a maximum of the surface area along the façades and offering 360° views of the surroundings.

The complex as a whole results in a residential building with a functional base that gets lighter as it gains in height.

_ZENIT TOWER

The facade is based on energetic efficiency, acoustics, and its integration into the Pyrenean landscape, looking for the most optimal orientation in order to enjoy the natural light and beautiful views of the landscape.

Multiuses Landscape & Urban

The Zenit Tower offers a sustainable approach with maximum comfort for its residents and users.

Visual relationships with the exterior are enhanced by arranging a maximum of the surface area along the façades.

SPINNER TOWER CAMPUS
SPAIN

The Spinner Tower Campus is a proposal for the university housing competition located in the city of Zaragoza. The project consists on a set of 504 homes grouped in 12 towers where the spaces of meeting and cohabitation are maximized.

On the ground floor of the towers there are four identical buildings with a triangular layout, but with different orientations. This floor is where the access to the towers and the campus shops are located. The interstitial space between buildings is occupied by a parking lot ventilated in a natural way. The first floor has been designed as a large garden for the tower inhabitants, a huge platform that connects the four buildings giving place to a space of leisure and other establishments which promote community life. The four residential towers are erected from the first floor onwards, each of them with seven floors and seven houses each floor. The configuration of the floor responds to a radial shape around a central atrium which allows natural ventilation, concentrating the services and the rooms in the central zone to maximize the living space-dining room-studio thus achieving that this space opens up to the façade.

The modulation of the residencies allows to achieve multiple options of distribution of the floor, which will be formally translated onto the façade. This, together with the non-orthogonal layout of the towers gives place to a set of great richness, observable from any perspective or angle.

Twisted Mixed-use Lifestyle

2-8 FLOOR
HOUSING
Private space

Tower building with 42 housing units of 37 and 30 sq. mts.

1rst FLOOR
COMMON & SPORT AREAS
Semi-private space

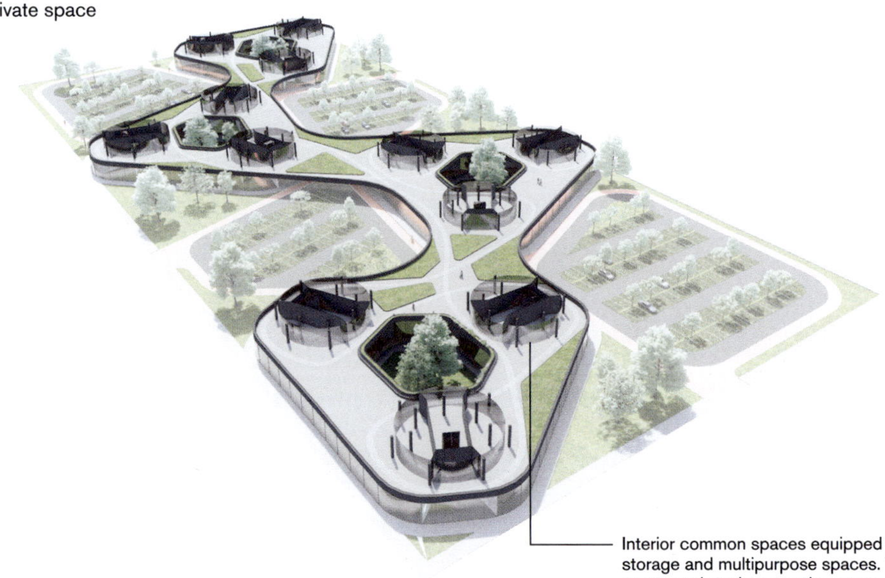

Interior common spaces equipped with laundry areas, storage and multipurpose spaces. The outdoor areas include sports and student meeting areas.

GROUND FLOOR
COMMERCE, PARKING, BICYCLE LANES
Public space

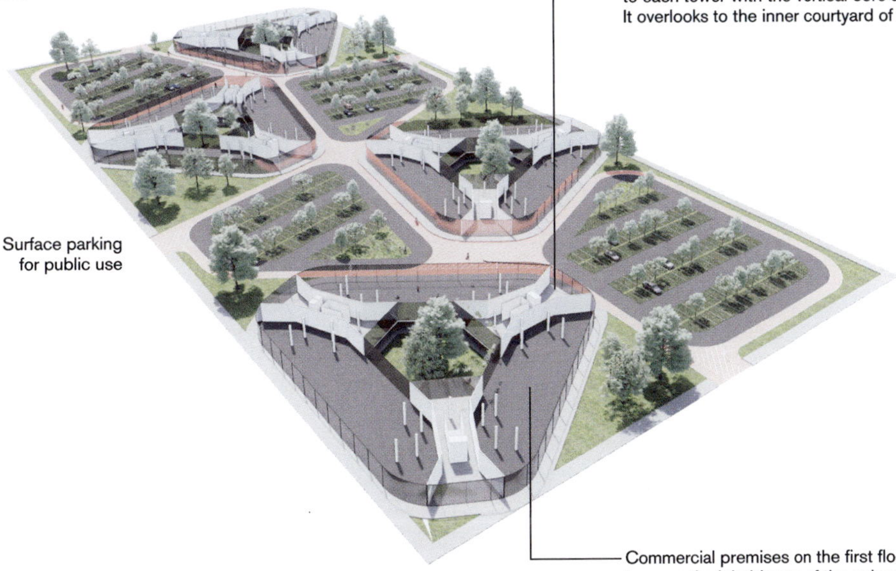

BASEMENT FLOOR
SUBWAY PARKING TOWERS
Private space

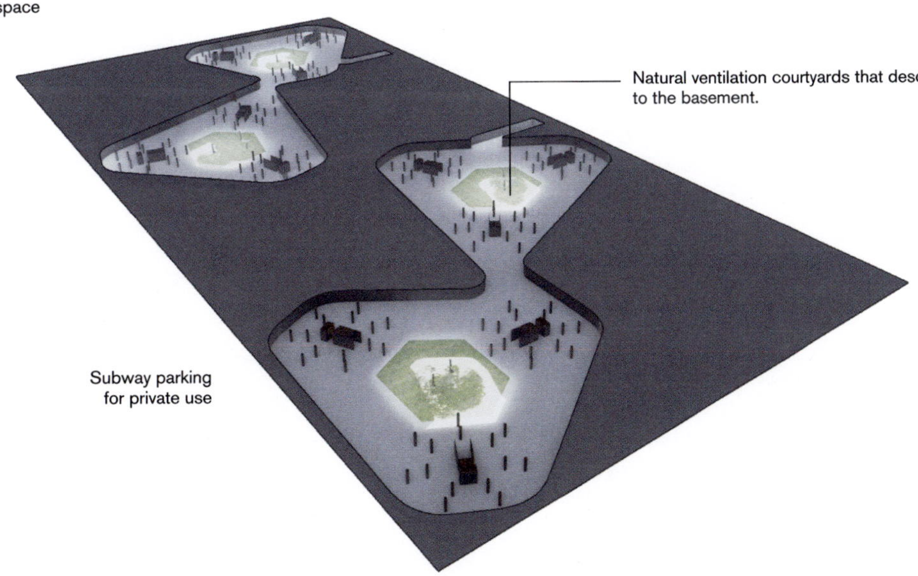

_SPINNER TOWER CAMPUS

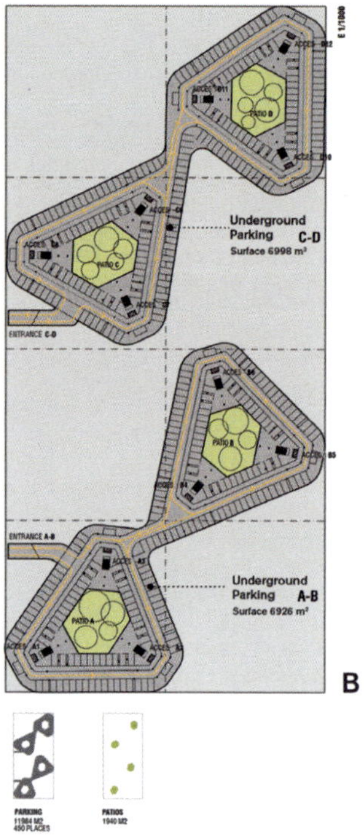

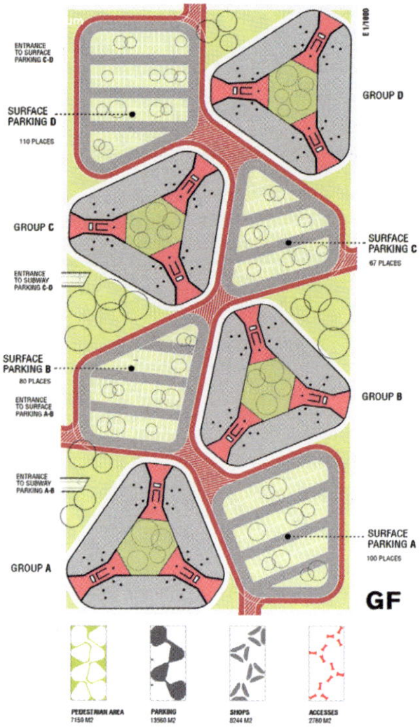

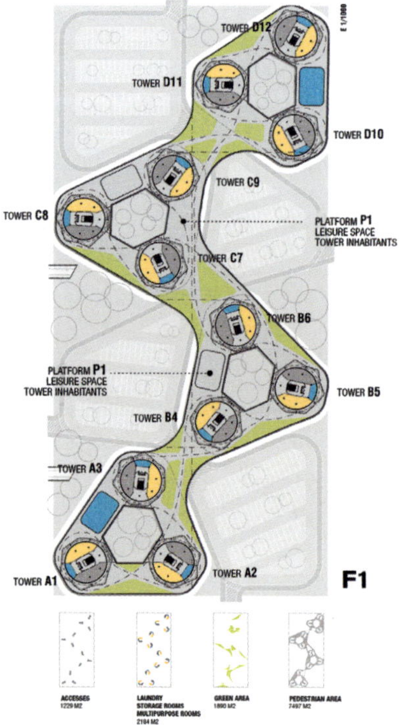

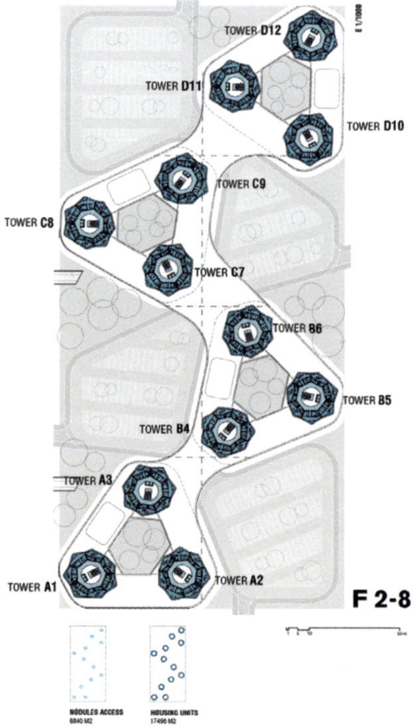

The space between triangular buildings is used to place a parking area. Another underground parking will air out naturally thanks to the disposition of courtyards.

The first floor is a garden for the inhabitants, a vast platform to establish a connection between the buildings as well as providing a leisure area where students can coexist.

HOUSING $37m^2$

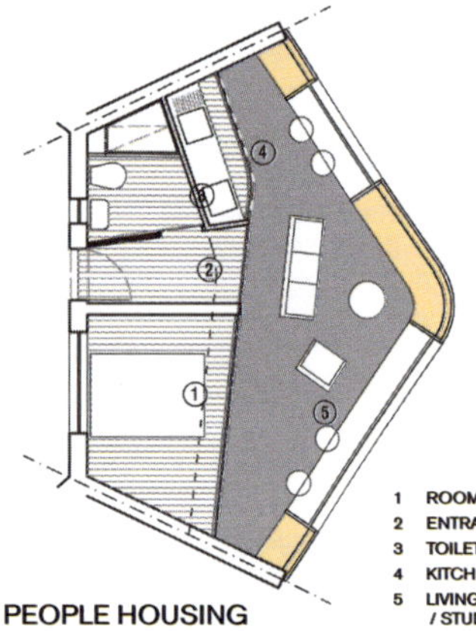

USABLE SURFACES

1	ROOM	7.61 M2
2	ENTRANCE HALL	2.98 M2
3	TOILET	3.30 M2
4	KITCHEN	2.27 M2
5	LIVING/DINING ROOM / STUDIO	19.67 M2

TWO PEOPLE HOUSING
(double room)

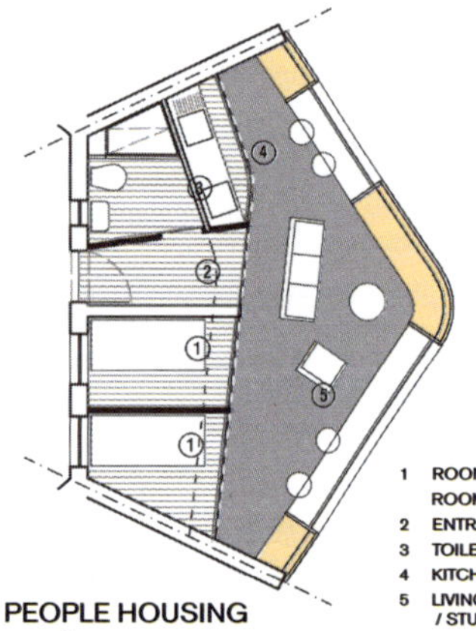

USABLE SURFACES

1	ROOM 1	3.68 M2
	ROOM 2	3.76 M2
2	ENTRANCE HALL	2.98 M2
3	TOILET	3.30 M2
4	KITCHEN	2.27 M2
5	LIVING/DINING ROOM / STUDIO	19.67 M2

TWO PEOPLE HOUSING
(two rooms)

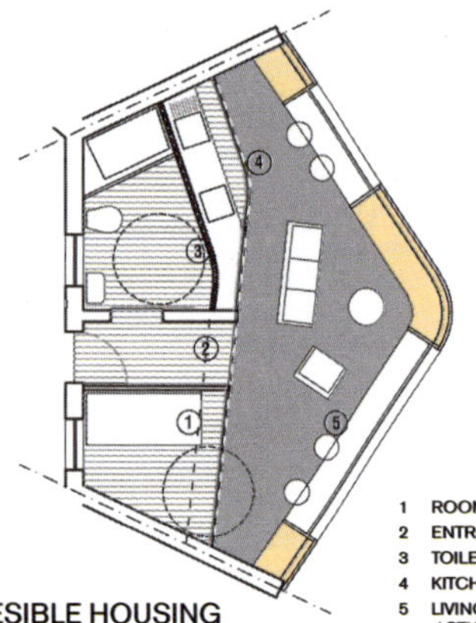

USABLE SURFACES

1	ROOM	4.81 M2
2	ENTRANCE HALL	2.80 M2
3	TOILET	5.71 M2
4	KITCHEN	2.89 M2
5	LIVING/DINING ROOM / STUDIO	19.67 M2

ACCESIBLE HOUSING
(one room)

HOUSING $30m^2$

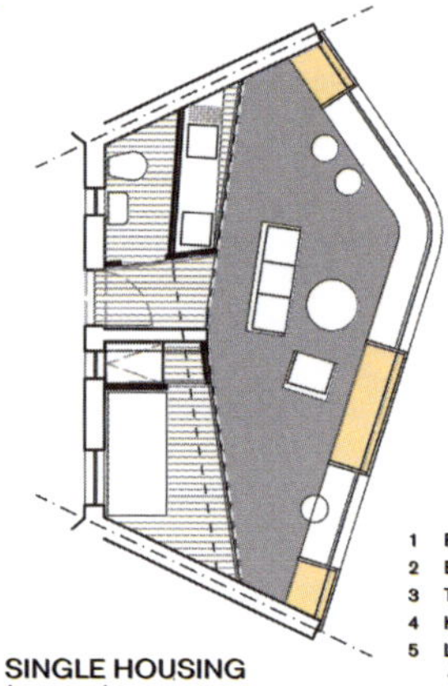

USABLE SURFACES

1	ROOM	5.74 M2
2	ENTRANCE HALL	1.89 M2
3	TOILET	2.11 M2
4	KITCHEN	1.88 M2
5	LIVING/DINING ROOM / STUDIO	19.55 M2

SINGLE HOUSING
(one room)

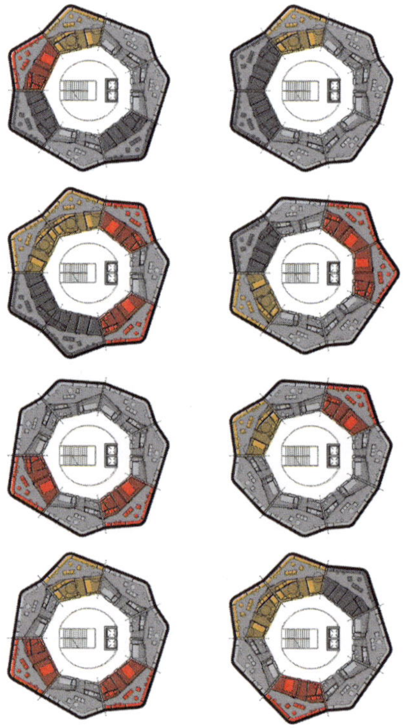

COMBINATION PLANTS
(examples of possible plant combinations)

The apartments distribution responds to a radial scheme around an atrium, allowing natural ventilation and containing the common services.

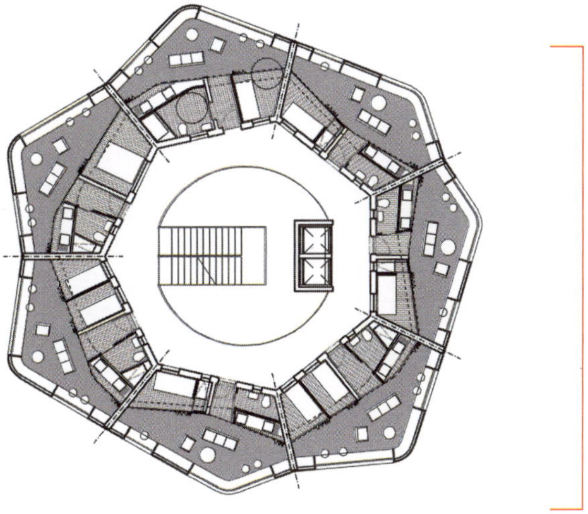

EXAMPLE TOWER PLANT E 1/200

TOWER PROFILES
(different profiles of the same tower depending on the point of view)

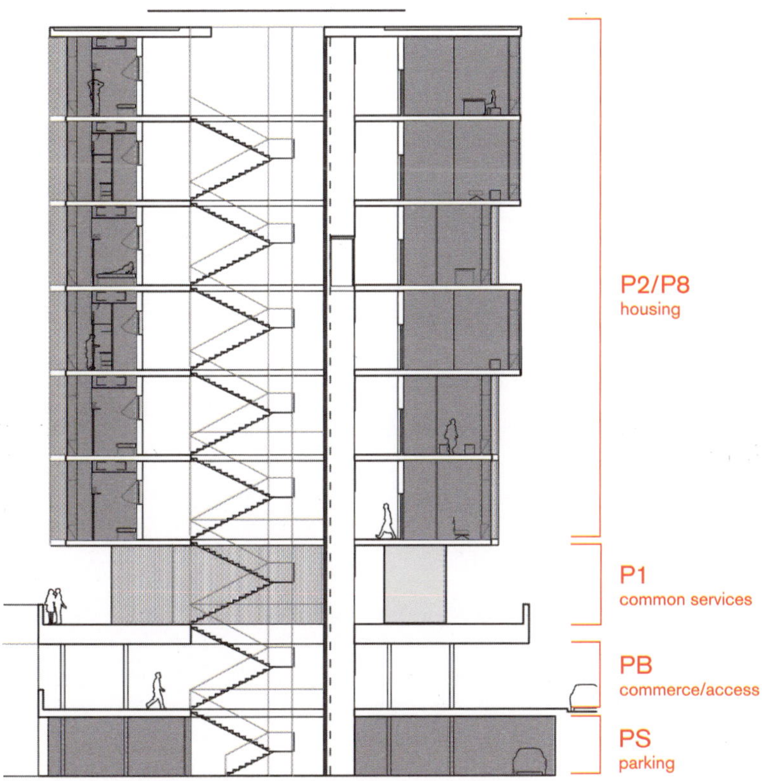

TOWER SECTION E 1/100

Researching and innovating with materials and building techniques related to parametric design is one of ON-A's main goals.

Regardless of the project's scale and its complex geometries, ON-A is committed to standardization, precision and, therefore, efficiency in the construction process.

Technology
Materials & Techniques

RICARDO_ Which project marked your beginning with technological research and material innovation? How do you connect that with design innovation?

JORDI_ The 5 Sentidos Lounge Bar didn't incorporate huge technological advances, but it did involve constructive and spatial innovation. Laser cutting was being used in architecture at the time, but just for railings, gates and enclosures. For a process like what we did in our design, with all the different pieces, it was quite unusual. In fact, the company that helped us normally does laser cutting for industrial parts. So, we hired a manufacturer outside the construction sector to handle those pieces.

5 Sentidos Lounge Bar, Girona. **--See page 64--**

EDUARDO_ The software we used was Rhino, but at the time its architectural applications were largely undeveloped. It was mainly used in jewelry and industrial design. Applying it to architecture was also an innovation.

RICARDO It's important for ON-A to design buildings using a limited number of materials and with clear innovation in their implementation. Was that also how you developed the design for Cricursa for Construmat? What was the potential of using curved glass?

JORDI For Cricursa, we took a different approach. It was a pavilion that could be dismantled, the type of structure that can be accumulated, assembled and disassembled. So, we used straight bars, with an "L" profile, and the nodes that connected them. That's how we generated the structure to support the curved glass, which also held the entire pavilion together. The material innovation was by Cricursa: spherical glass, curved glass, folded glass, large-format glass, etched glass. Our goal was for the stand to reflect all the company's technical possibilities. There was a study done on the possibilities, and we tried to push them to the limit. In the end, the sensation was like being inside a giant glass geode. We also wanted to create a poetic metaphor for silica, as the natural origin of glass.

RICARDO In which other projects have you pushed other materials to the limit or experimented with their form and their installation?

JORDI **We've always kept material and technical innovation in mind.**

The Drassanes Metro Station was also a benchmark, since the walls, the ceiling and the pavements were all pushed to the limit to generate a continuous envelope. We try to simplify solutions using just a few materials. That's something we always keep in mind at ON-A, although later it may generate complexity in terms of geometry and shapes. The Smart Mesh Building and the Pattern Building projects, although they may seem complex, actually use the same mesh with different degrees of openness and a single construction solution from top to bottom.

EDUARDO **The Drassanes Metro Station is a very good example of how many different aspects can be resolved using a single material (in this case GRC):** the junction between the walls and the floor, the ventilation grids, the benches, the ceilings (which are mobile to provide access to the building services, using a simple counterweight), or the anchor points for the light fixtures on the platforms. The entire station was built using just five molds. Ultimately, it's an envelope that works for everything.

Sant Pau Cultural Center, Tarragona.

RICARDO Could you explain how you used a lightweight material like ETFE as a roof for Sant Pau Cultural Center?

EDUARDO In that case, we were trying to arrive at two solutions: the existing construction couldn't support much weight, so we had to make a roof as light as possible and protect the interior monument of the Sant Pau chapel, plus we also had to let some natural light in. We opted for ETFE because it offered all the right conditions. Using glass would have been very expensive and heavy.

JORDI We always start with the search for the right material so that it meets all the requirements of the project, and if we have to innovate in the implementation, we try to find a manufacturer who wants to join in our experimentation.

The zinc we used in the roof for Sant Pau Cultural Center was built with a manufacturer who is an expert in the material. We like to work with industrialists who are willing to take risks, knowing about their technique, their technology, and trying to go one step further and push them to the limit.

The industrialist who did the 5 Sentidos Bar Lounge had never done anything like it, but we did all the work with him: verifying the geometry, making the cuts, building a prototype, investigating the nodes, the points of connection for each piece, etc. For the Drassanes station, there was also a challenge with how to bring all the pieces into the station, which was still operational, via the tracks at night. Or how many pieces could be transported on each track.

Sant Pau Cultural Center, Tarragona.

RICARDO You choose a material for its features, because it responds to a series of conditions (load, use, etc.) and also because of sustainability issues. How do you balance all those conditions, without sacrificing a certain aesthetic? How does the installation of those materials influence the building's ultimate form?

EDUARDO Basically, the idea is to choose a material and adapt it to the needs of the project, and work with it using the existing technology so that it works the way we want it to.

JORDI This type of parametric architecture, with different pieces and complex geometries, inevitably entails an industrialization process. All these pieces account for the molds, the divisions, trying to bring the process into the workshop to create this type of architecture. The single-family home in Barcelona —Panoramic House— is all built with different pieces of GRC. Obviously, you need to have accurate 3D modeling. Then you work with an industrialist who can take that model, read it and generate molds from it. And then make sure the pieces come from the workshop in perfect condition to fit together on the site. In another single-family house in Barcelona —Pre-fab House—, everything is industrialized: the structure is made of wood and was designed using the Revit program, which was transposed into the software used by the lightweight timber framing company. The calculations were done there, with all the pieces for the frames and the struts. The shell and the structure were assembled in under a week (you can watch the video of the assembly on the ON-A website).

This kind of architecture requires industrial processes that make the execution of the work faster, more efficient and therefore more sustainable.

The most significant areas include the Sant Pau cloister, with its chapel dating from the 13th century, now protected under a new roof with an organic, structural matrix that shows off a unique geometry. A series of skylights lets in natural light through domes made from high-resistance plastic membranes.

Sant Pau Cultural Center, Tarragona.

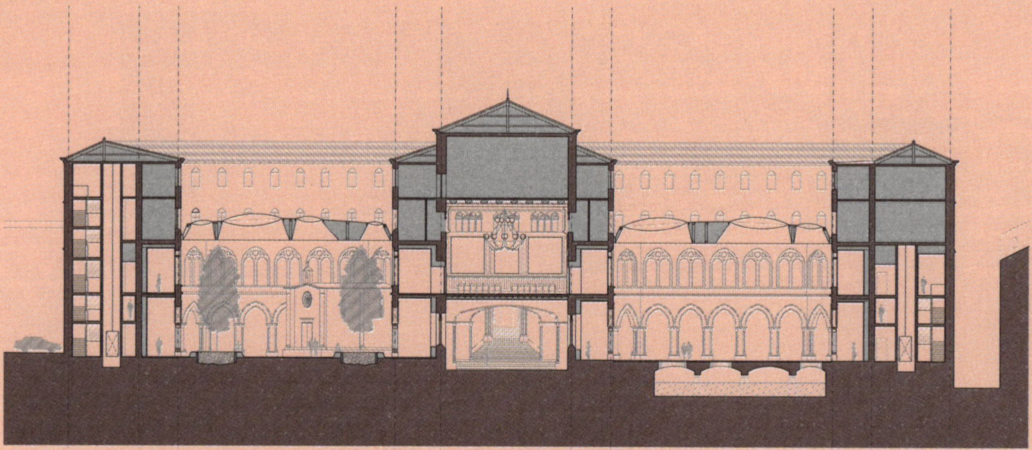

Integration
Structural Matrix
Heritage

Sant Pau Cultural Center, Tarragona.

RICARDO You have projects with different uses but, especially, with different scales. You can make a small pavilion for a trade fair or a skyscraper, a park or even a city. In this whole process that you've been talking about with pre-construction and ad hoc construction for each design, how is the change in scale important? Does it imply a radical change in the construction process of how you build your projects?

EDUARDO I don't think so. When you have digital control of a geometry that you can send to an industrialist to manufacture for you, he doesn't care if there are three or 30,000 pieces. The installation process is different: the timing isn't the same, but once you have a clear idea of what the piece is like and how it will be placed, it's just a matter of time. For the Drassanes Metro Station we had 210 pieces on the platforms, two types of pieces, and depending on how they were manufactured they were installed on site. The pieces had to be a specific size and weight so that the crane on the track could be maneuvered between two people. That meant that the pieces had to be 1.20 m wide. If the installation technique at the time hadn't been able to handle the weight, the pieces would have been 0.60 m, and as a result the construction or its final appearance would have been different. If a bigger size had been possible, maybe we could have used four-meter-wide pieces. Everything has to be planned out in the control of the geometry and the assembly. The same thing happened with the Lounge Bar. And with the façade of the Mataró houses —El Rengle Tower—, where installing a piece on the first floor was different from the 14th floor. In that case, a piece on the first floor could be five times bigger than one on the 14th, but when it came to standardization so the same molds could be used, we used the one that would be most difficult install, and from there we standardized the rest of the parts.

El Rengle Tower, Barcelona.

The construction systems used in this building aim for the optimization and improvement of habitual construction systems. For the façade, the use of industrialized elements was prioritized, giving prominence to curved GRC panels with different geometries.

El Rengle Tower, Barcelona.

This detached house is set out lengthwise over its plot in a construction comprising two stories. The most singular of these overhangs shelters the outside living room, an open-air space that connects at the front with the terrace-solarium and pool.

Panoramic House, Barcelona.

The body of the ground floor juts out in space in a subtle overhang that gives strength to the architecture with lateral folds that accentuate the dual directions of the structure's overall design.

Panoramic house, Barcelona.

RICARDO How do you use more traditional materials? Have you ever considered using brick? And if you did, can you imagine how you might protocolize their installation?

EDUARDO Right now, you can use bricks in two ways: how they've been laid for as long as anyone can remember, or using a robotic arm to lay the bricks with digitally controlled angles and geometries. We'd use bricks if that were the case. Otherwise, it doesn't offer us anything, and we aren't attracted to using them just because. Although we haven't had the occasion up to now, we are equipped to design and innovate with them.

JORDI The façade of the apartment building in Empuriabrava —Pattern Building— could actually be built using a robot, giving it instructions for where each piece would go, so it could place them precisely. Again, everything would have to be encoded.

RICARDO To what extent do you consider vegetation, plants ("greenery") to be an architectural material? How do you incorporate it into your projects?

JORDI We've always treated "greenery" like a material, because of its advantages both in terms of climate control and insulation, etc. Plus, there's the aspect of biophilia – people's need for contact and connection with nature.

That's something that has always been an undercurrent at ON-A, since our first competition. Working with technological partners, we're investigating the use of greenery as an efficient material, to make it sustainable, for example, by reducing water consumption. We're doing tests with prototypes, using different types of plants and substrates, which give us reliable data on the benefits that greenery can offer on façades while complying with CTE standards and other regulations. We've studied the prototypes over the course of a year, in different climates.

EDUARDO The Algeciras Seafront —LLano Amarillo Park— competition was foundational in terms of working with the landscape and using vegetation as a design material. We defined the encoding for the plants, choosing the species according to the slopes and the orientation with respect to the sea. We used the resulting plan in different colors, which laid out the use of the green material.

It was like a blueprint for laying paving tiles, but instead of tiles they were plants and trees.

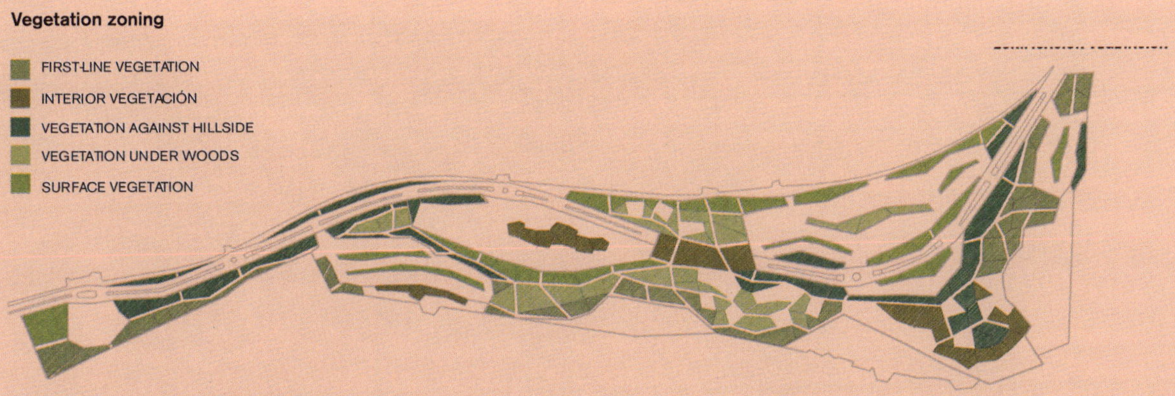

Llano Amarillo Park, Algeciras.
--See page 89--

Restructuring the Camp Clar sports complex for the celebration of the 2018 Mediterranean Games involves planning for two realities: the first during the games; and the second after the games are over, when the program must be consolidated into the creation of a large sports park.

Mediterranean Games Masterplan, Tarragona.

How the space could be used after the games and how the facilities would be maintained was our main goal. To that effect, it was decided that the infrastructures that could not ensure long-term profitability would be temporary, for use only during the games. Facilities that could be repurposed, such as the sports center, would be permanent.

Mediterranean Games Masterplan, Tarragona.

RICARDO Do you think everything you learned about construction at the Barcelona School of Architecture empowered you to take this leap in your designs and use materials in this way? Or, if not, what do you think the approach to teaching construction should be?

JORDI When we were studying, the technical and construction training was very strong compared to other schools in the world. It was a differentiating factor, but it was approached from a very traditional and conservative point of view. That may be different now or, at least, with the appearance of private schools, like the IAAC, it may be taught in a different way. When we were in school, innovation in materials was not encouraged. But, in our work with Enric Ruiz-Geli on Cloud 9 and then in Eduardo's work with Jean Nouvel and Alejandro Zaera, the contact with more innovative architects showed us another way of understanding architecture.

Obviously, that baggage in terms of construction and technical knowledge is always there, and it has been useful as a foundation and in understanding the layers of an architectural envelope. But the research on façades is something we've done outside of school.

EDUARDO In general, our professors designed to suit traditional construction methods, and they didn't go beyond that. What I did see, for example, in Nouvel's studio, was a department dedicated to engineering applications in architecture. In the initial stages of a design idea, we always tried to test how it might be built in the future. There were people responsible for that process who had the knowledge and experience, who were in contact with industrialists, and who were aware of the latest technologies in construction and manufacturing. Of course, it surprises me that something similar doesn't exist in schools, where future architects are being taught. That's why at ON-A we also have an R&D department for innovation in materials, techniques and geometries.

JORDI We actively look for companies that can develop that type of architecture or digital manufacturing techniques.

Every Friday, we have a guest presenter come to the office to teach us about innovations in different fields. It's true that that's something we learned at school from Professor Alfons Soldevilla, the advisor on our final degree projects. He was the only architect at the school who experimented. In fact, we chose him because he was different: implementing innovation in program, in form and its geometries, in construction techniques and in materials. The project I proposed was an inflatable building. With any other advisor at the school, it would have been unthinkable.

RICARDO Can you tell us who your technology partners tend to be?

JORDI A lot of companies consult with us, but above all we value industrialists or companies that are involved with innovation and research, and who want to push their work to the limit, hand in hand with us. Also, people who like the creative aspect of developing things they've never done before. That was our experience with the metalworker Ramon Presa for the 5 Sentidos Lounge Bar. He's an enthusiast, who knows his trade very well, but he takes almost an artistic approach. We've also collaborated with Cricursa, a company dedicated to ongoing innovation in architectural glass. Verdtical is another of our technological partners, for architectural greenery. There's also Cubs, a technology company that deals with architecture designed using BIM and with building management. Culleré Sala is a metal structure company with an element of engineering and research; we did the roof of the Seminary of Tarragona with them. Arquima is the company that did the wooden house in Sant Cugat —Pre-fab House—. They also helped us with the prototype for the house with the green roof. For the façades of the residential building in Mataró, we collaborated with Planas Ark, a company that makes GRC elements and architectural concrete. They're also involved in research and they support unique projects. In fact, after Mataró we did a project in Sabadell.

There are two kinds of industrialists: the kind who love their work and want to move forward and progress, and the kind who are fine with what they're already doing and have no need to move beyond that. Both attitudes are perfectly legitimate, but we probably won't be working with the second kind, because we're interested in the others. Like we were saying, we set ourselves certain innovation challenges at the firm, although we don't have a specific department for it. That's why we look for technological partners.

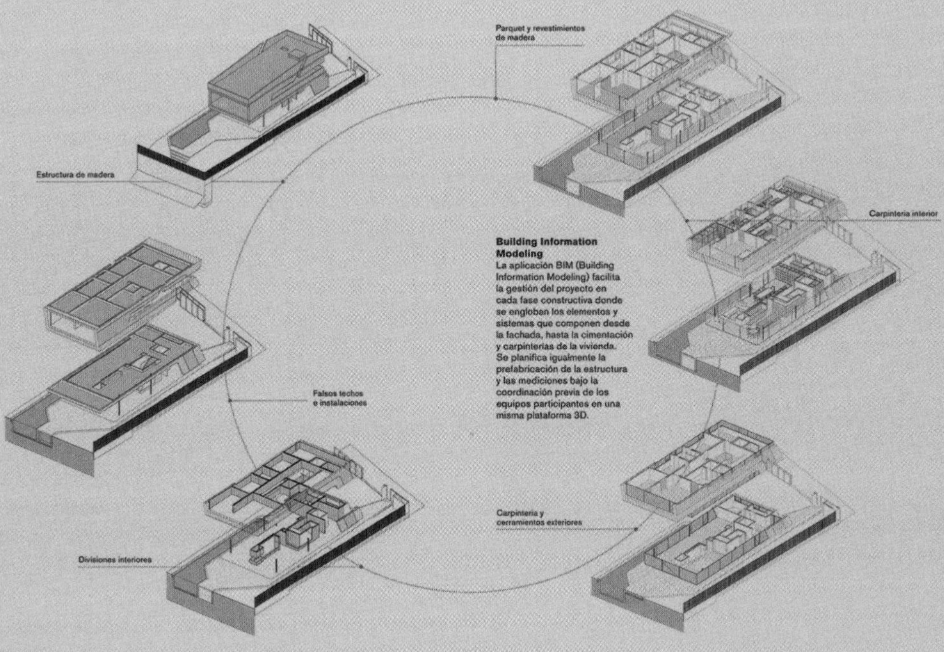

Pre-fab House, Barcelona.

Pre-fab House, Barcelona.

ETERIC RESIDENTIAL
BARCELONA

The land-use planning project for an area on the seafront is the context for a study on the most efficient development solution, looking into the co-existence of social housing, rent-controlled housing and market-rate housing typologies in the same building. The distribution is organized according to uses, situating the market-rate units in the most valuable areas of the building.

It is a new construction project of 119 homes in two building volumes (69 homes on plot 6.1 and 50 homes on plot 6.2), underground parking for 131 car spaces, 24 motorcycle spaces and 119 storage rooms, located in the sector PMU of Mataró, Maresme region. The project consists of two residential volumes, a large green area and a low body, housing a total of 119 homes with 4, 3 and 2 bedrooms.

Each block is located at a different elevation and is distributed through a central core. All counters and technical rooms are located in their respective lobby areas. On the roof of the linear block, there will be a communal pool, and the one in the tower is destined to the private terraces of the immediately lower houses. The common space of the urbanization has been designed in order to offer a better quality of life to the inhabitants, enjoying green spaces and outdoor activities. The garden has a swimming pool, solarium, hammock area, children's playground with games and green areas. The interior routes are accessible to give access to the two buildings. In the center, a paved platform houses the pool, protected by a controlled perimeter for children. The proposal includes the planting of several trees that give this space privacy while offering shade for the hottest days.

PONENT

The common space of the urbanization has been designed in order to offer a better quality of life to the inhabitants, enjoying green spaces and outdoor activity.

Community Balconies Greenery

The garden has a swimming pool, solarium, hammock area, children's playground with games and green areas.

All rooms stand out for their distribution, are bright and spacious, with of modern and functional finishes.

All homes have space for the natural and mechanical drying of clothes, as well as space for personal and general storage.

ETERIC

The distribution is organized according to uses, situating the market-rate units in the most valuable areas of the building.

MATARÓ PORT HOTEL
BARCELONA

Equipped with an excellent location, on the seafront in the coastal city of Mataró (Barcelona), it has been designed to be able to always take advantage of the privileged views of the place, both from the room terraces and from the cover.

The layout of the building allude to nautical motifs, reminiscent of a yacht due to its unique shape and arrangement. This bold and daring image is achieved by prioritizing the use of industrialized and modular elements. The incorporation of LED strips that run through the entire volume, help to reinforce the dynamism of the composition, and give it presence and visibility in its nighttime perception.

It has a capacity of 150 rooms distributed in a total of six floors, with surfaces that vary between 20 sqm and 70 sqm. All the rooms are equipped with a complete bathroom and a small office-kitchen and have large terraces with views of the Mediterranean Sea. The roof of the building, has a large infinity pool and a Skybar.

Regarding sustainability, the design of the terrace running along the entire perimeter of the building will allow for control of sunlight throughout the year. This, added to the use of materials with high energy efficiency and the connection to an urban air conditioning network (the Tub Verd Mataró network), will make this aparthotel a building with almost zero consumption.

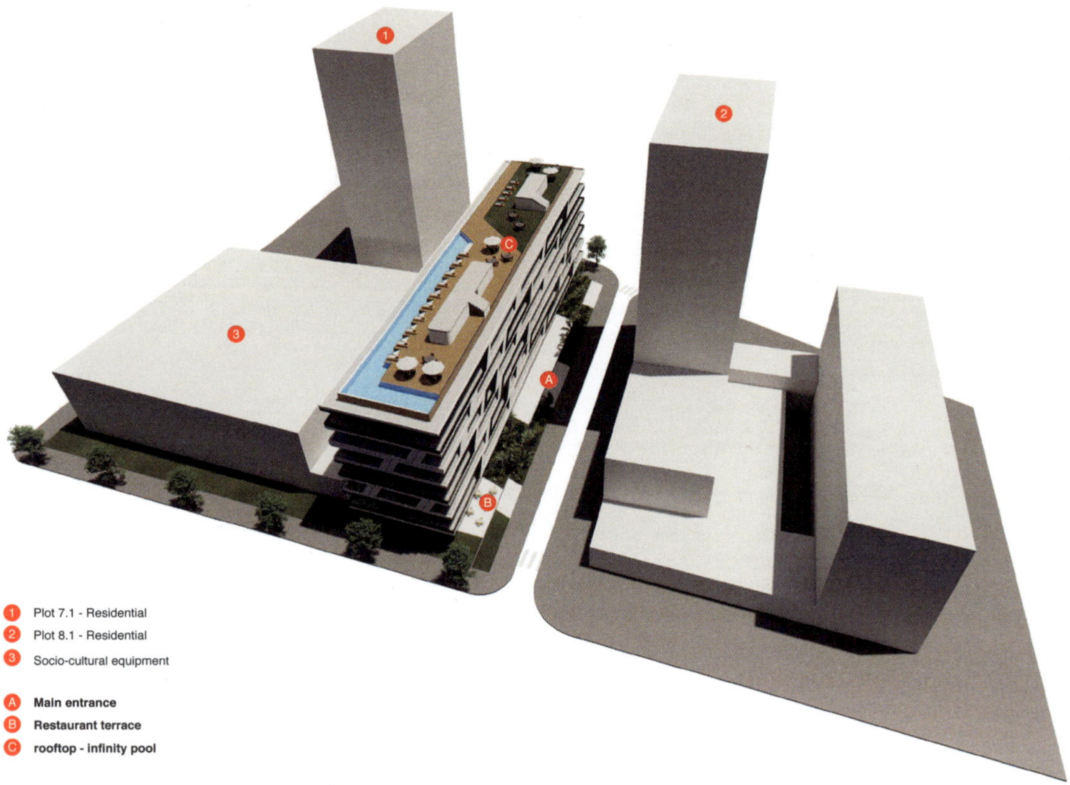

1 Plot 7.1 - Residential
2 Plot 8.1 - Residential
3 Socio-cultural equipment

A **Main entrance**
B **Restaurant terrace**
C **rooftop - infinity pool**

Lyfestile
Light
Uniqueness

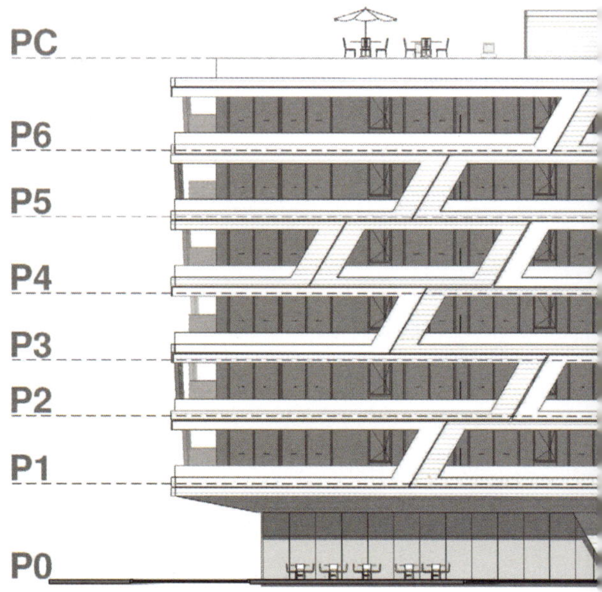

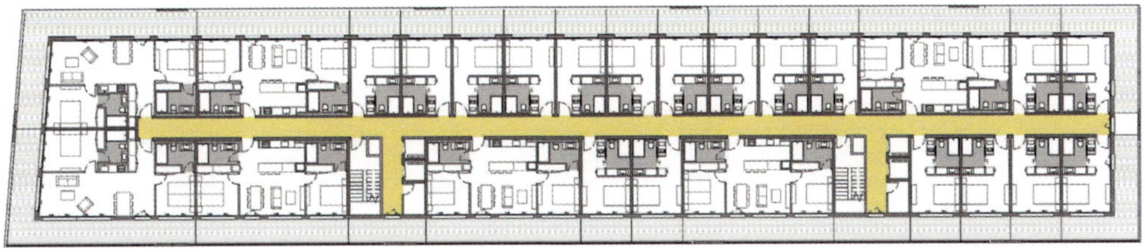

P1 a P6 Rooms

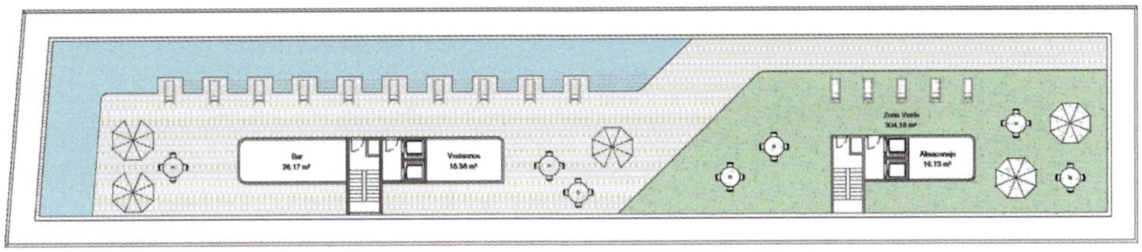

PC Roof-top

Access to the building is located on the first floor. 150 rooms are distributed over a total of six floors. The roof, as a boat, has a large infinity pool and a Skybar.

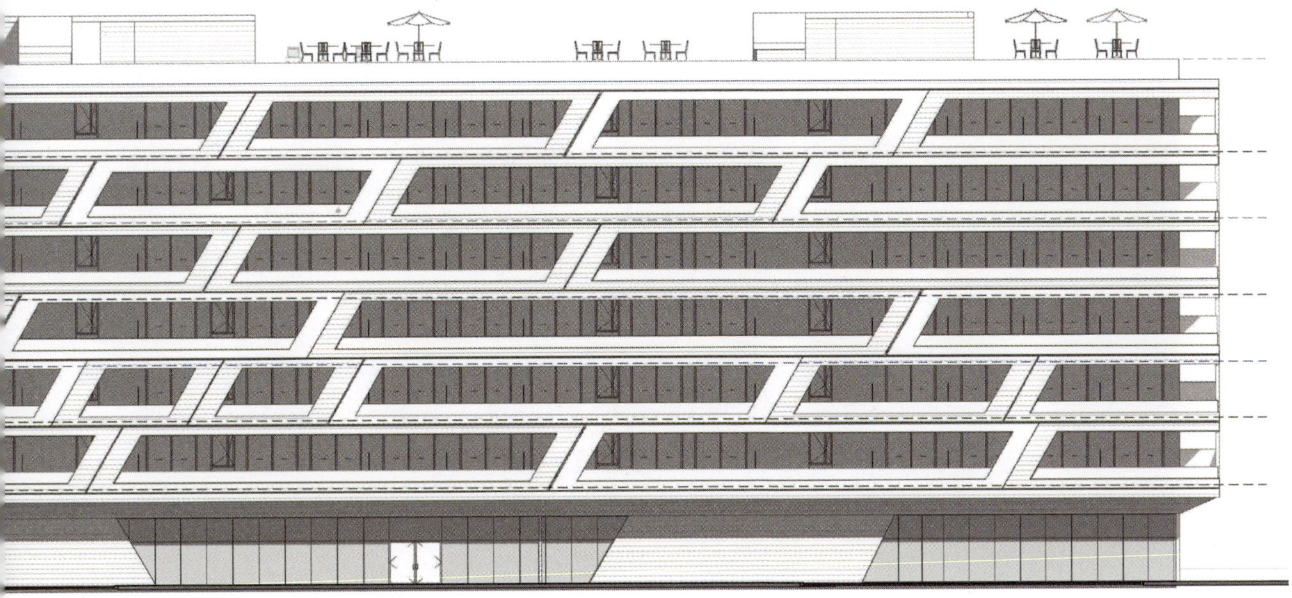

The dynamic layout of Mataró Port Hotel, and the aesthetics of the façade allude to nautical motifs, reminiscent of a yacht in its singular shape.

The roof space, and the balcony terraces, have been designed to offer a panoramic view of the fishing town of Mataró with the sea in the background.

POWER & LIGHT HOTEL
TAIPEI

Located in the Songshan District of Taipei, along one of the city's main avenues, this project is for a multi-use complex that includes housing, a hotel and commercial premises on the ground floor.

Technology and innovation come together to generate a building that is in keeping with our times. Following the profile of a hybrid building, a residential complex made up of two towers connects to the main volume – a hotel with commercial areas at its base. A technological envelope extends, uninterrupted, across the façades and pavements, lending the whole a certain architectural consistency.

The three volumes in the new complex are articulated by the same light envelope, which maintains a single architectural language despite the heterogeneity of the different buildings.

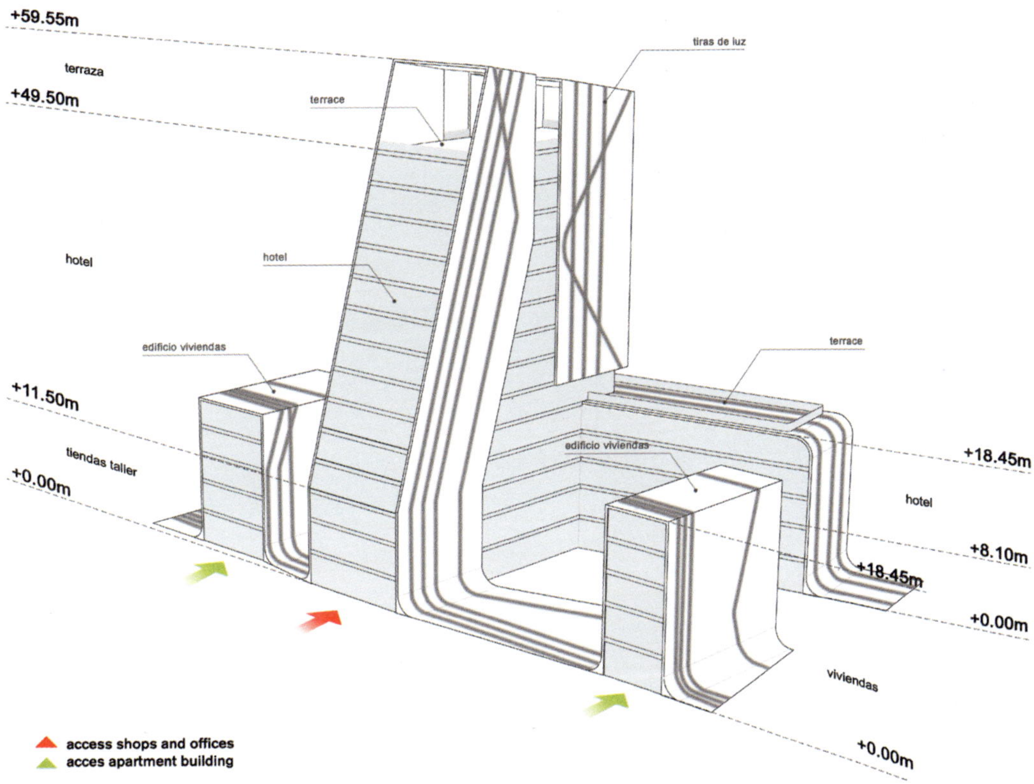

Three volumes are articulated under the same light mantle that amid its heterogeneity, retaining the same motif.

Continuity Light Envelope Multi-use

The hybrid building —a residential complex, a hotel, and commercial areas— is integrated within a futuristic layout materialized in a technological mantle that extends uninterruptedly along facades and pavements.

NEOM MEGA-CITY
SAUDI ARABIA

The NEOM city project originated with a proposal for the government of Saudi Arabia to create a new city on the Arabian Peninsula near the Sinai.
The city looks toward the future by basing its organization on technology, audiovisual experiences and communications.

The heart of the design is a city-shield, using geometric forms to create a shell to protect against the hot and hostile climate of Saudi Arabia. At the same time, the shield serves as an energy collector and offers solar protection, generating shade to help control the temperatures underneath.

Inside the city, the open-air spaces offer many green areas with gardens and meeting places that favor the development and maintenance of biophilia and help keep the air clean.

The city is not accessible by car; vehicles are parked outside, adjacent to a public transportation hub with a hyperloop. Movement within the city is allowed through car sharing or in driverless vehicles. The hyperloop also offers quick connections with other cities, such as Cairo.

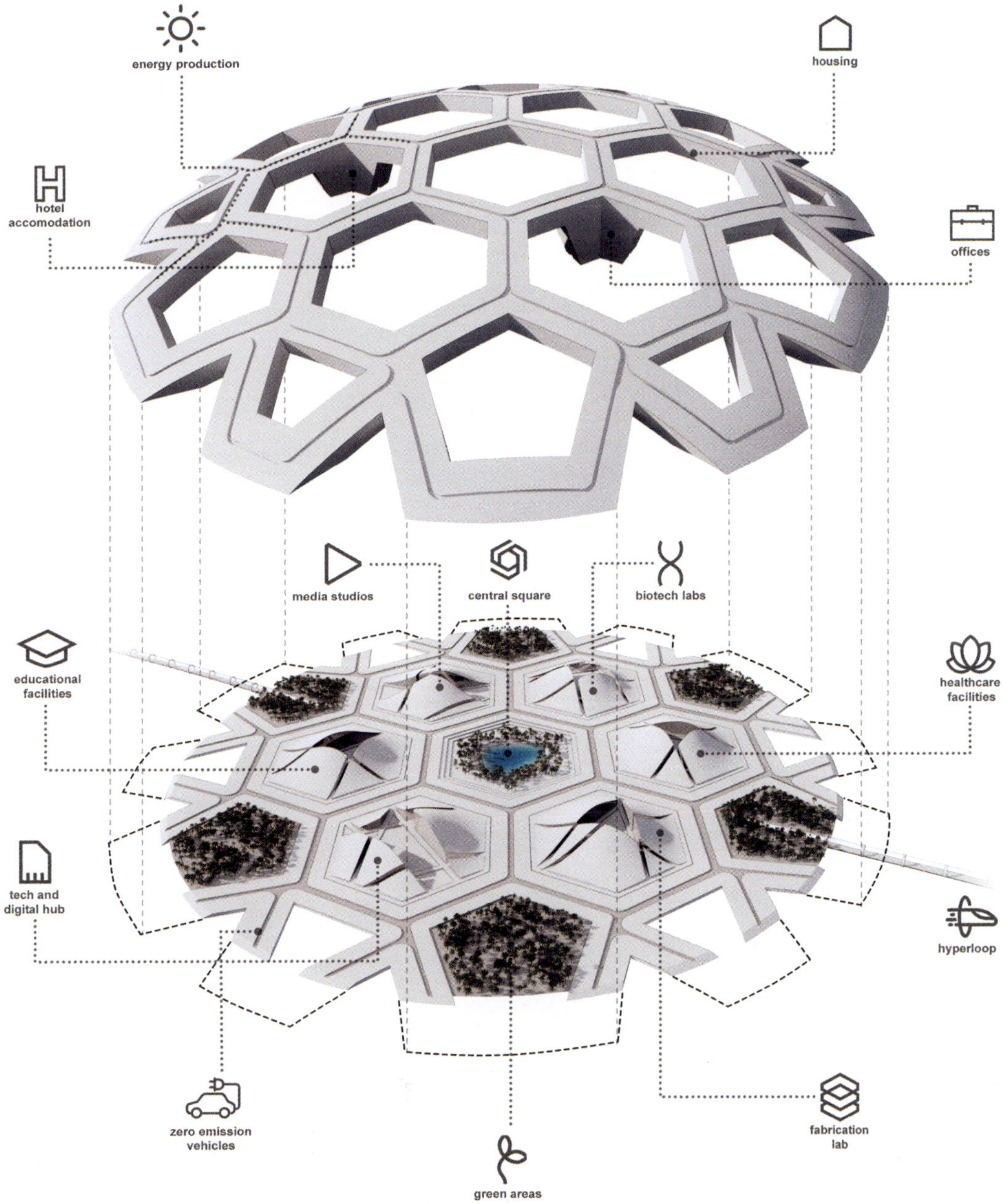

The city as a shell protects citizens against the hot and hostile climate, serves as an energy collector, and offers solar protection, generating shade to help control the temperatures underneath.

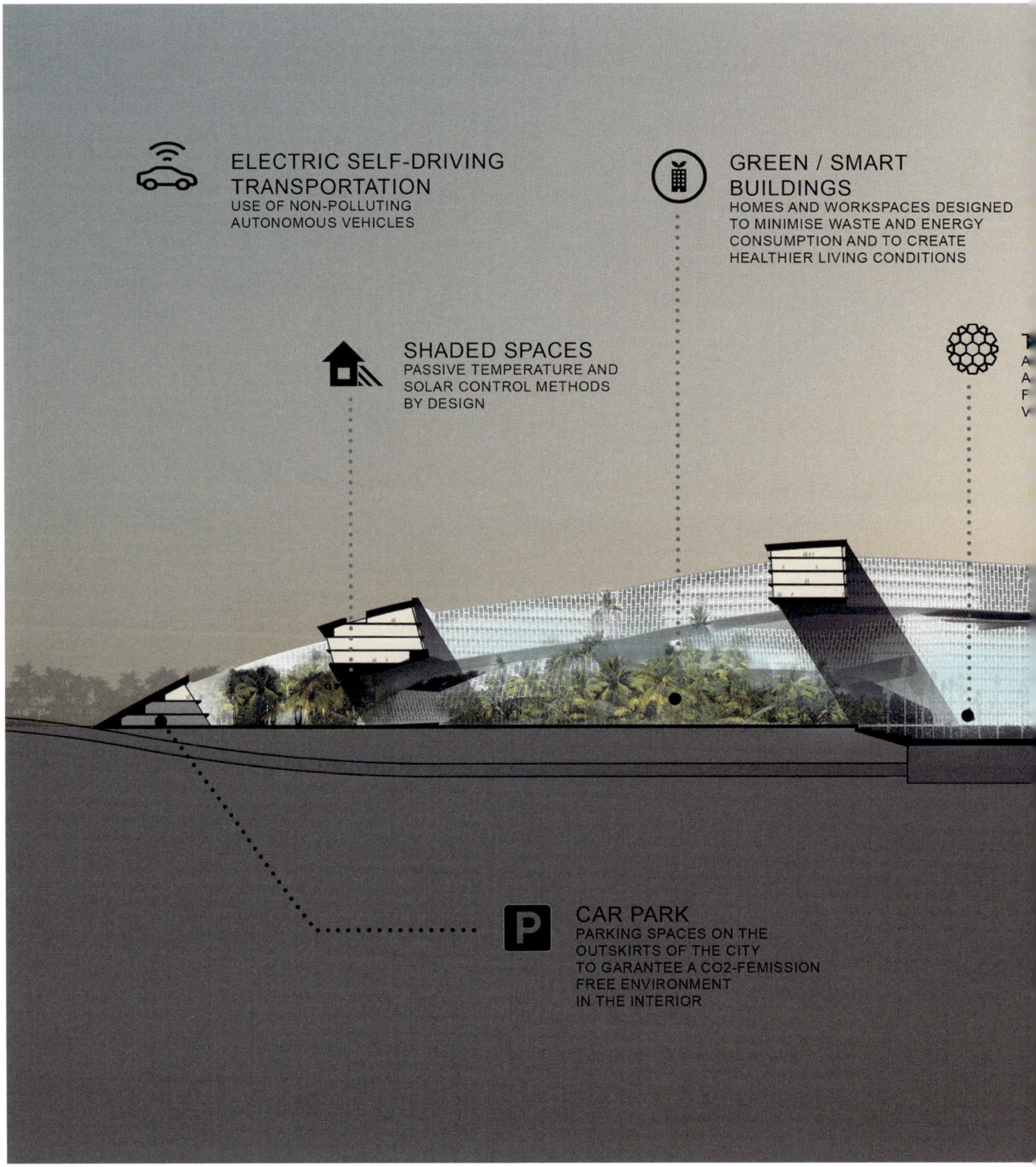
ELECTRIC SELF-DRIVING TRANSPORTATION
USE OF NON-POLLUTING AUTONOMOUS VEHICLES
GREEN / SMART BUILDINGS
HOMES AND WORKSPACES DESIGNED TO MINIMISE WASTE AND ENERGY CONSUMPTION AND TO CREATE HEALTHIER LIVING CONDITIONS
SHADED SPACES
PASSIVE TEMPERATURE AND SOLAR CONTROL METHODS BY DESIGN
CAR PARK
PARKING SPACES ON THE OUTSKIRTS OF THE CITY TO GARANTEE A CO2-FEMISSION FREE ENVIRONMENT IN THE INTERIOR

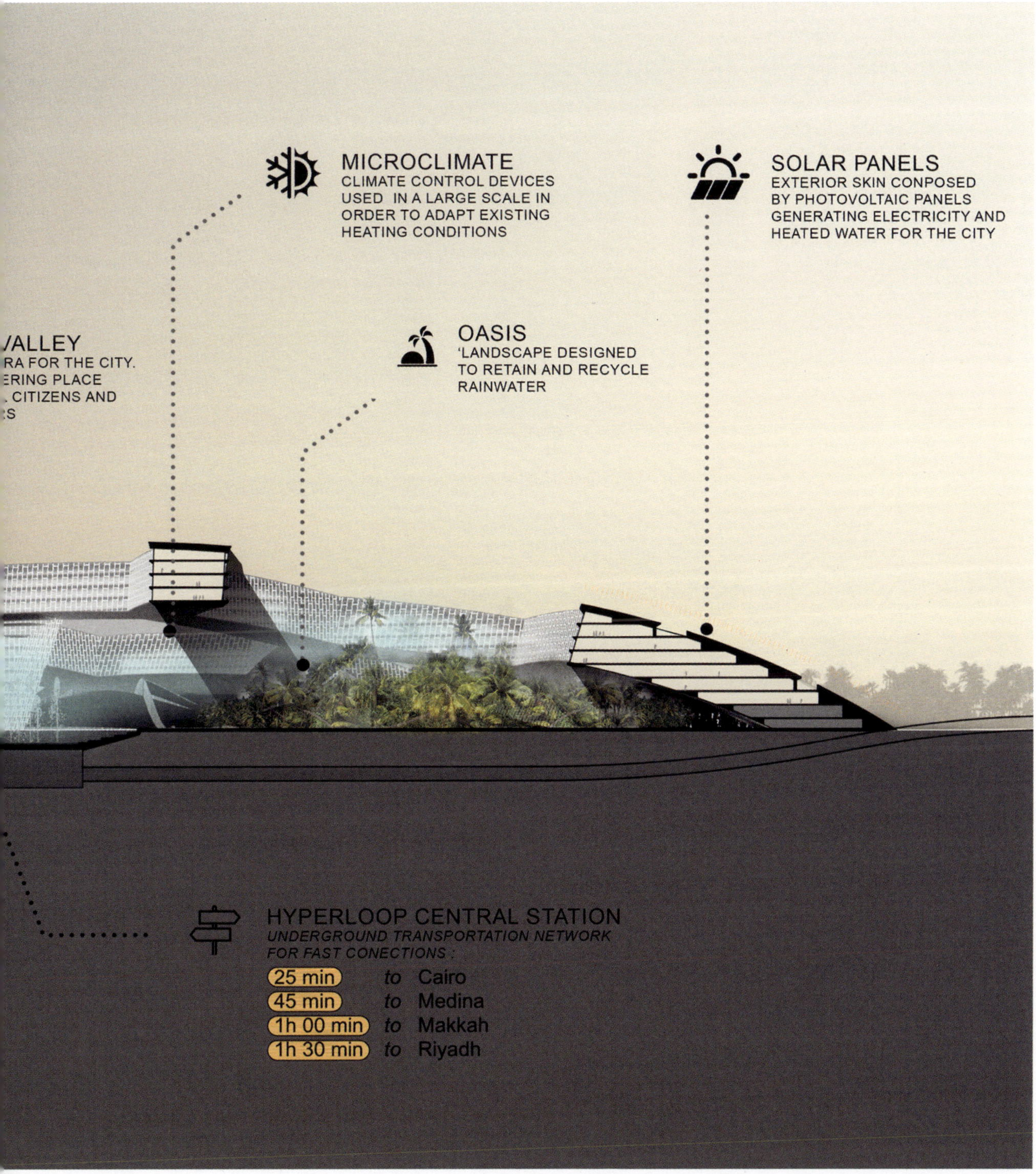
MICROCLIMATE
CLIMATE CONTROL DEVICES
USED IN A LARGE SCALE IN
ORDER TO ADAPT EXISTING
HEATING CONDITIONS
SOLAR PANELS
EXTERIOR SKIN CONPOSED
BY PHOTOVOLTAIC PANELS
GENERATING ELECTRICITY AND
HEATED WATER FOR THE CITY
/ALLEY
RA FOR THE CITY.
ERING PLACE
. CITIZENS AND
S
OASIS
'LANDSCAPE DESIGNED
TO RETAIN AND RECYCLE
RAINWATER
HYPERLOOP CENTRAL STATION
UNDERGROUND TRANSPORTATION NETWORK
FOR FAST CONECTIONS :
25 min to Cairo
45 min to Medina
1h 00 min to Makkah
1h 30 min to Riyadh

Private vehicles are parked outside, adjacent to a public transportation hub with a hyperloop. Movement within the city is allowed through car sharing or in driverless vehicles.

Shell
Compacity
Mobility
Efficiency

THANKS

By Eduardo Gutiérrez
and Jordi Fernández

After months of work and many hours of dialog with the editor of this monograph, Ricardo Devesa, we have collected in this book an important part of our ideas and projects of all the years of our career.

At ON-A we have work from the first day with the hope of contributing to society through our knowledge and dedication. In all this period, the conducting thread of our trajectory, the motor of our decisions and our main distinction has been the constant innovation in various fields. The ceaseless quest for new ways of projecting, of using new materials, of understanding new ways of inhabiting spaces, of upgrading the design and construction processes and of learning and keeping on providing innovative solutions to the new challenges which the 21st century poses, have been our main leitmotiv.

However, nothing of what you have seen in this monograph would be possible without the implication of many actors. In this final chapter, we would like to give visibility and thank all of those who are part of our history and who are responsible, in part, for our work.

Firstly, we would like to thank our clients. Without them our work would not have meaning. During all these years we have worked with many companies, big and small, but behind each of them there were people who, in one way or another, have trusted us and have bet on ON-A as the firm where they could make their projects become a reality. Among many others we would like to highlight four of them who, for different reasons, have been fundamental for us: Evaristo Gallego, Jaume Pujol, Anna&Ivo and Luis Gil.

Residential
Housing
Developers

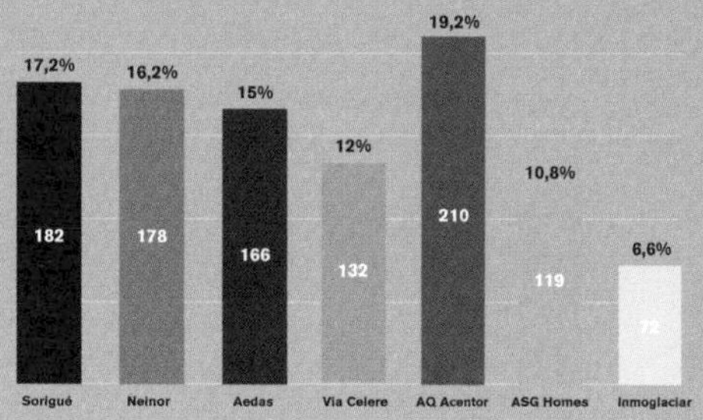

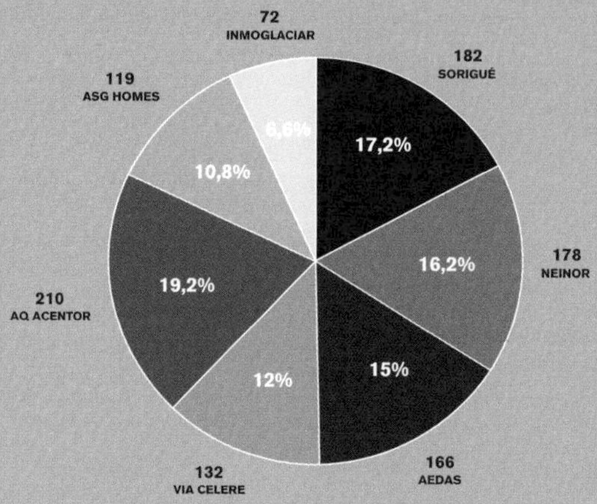

Residential
Built-up area
Developers

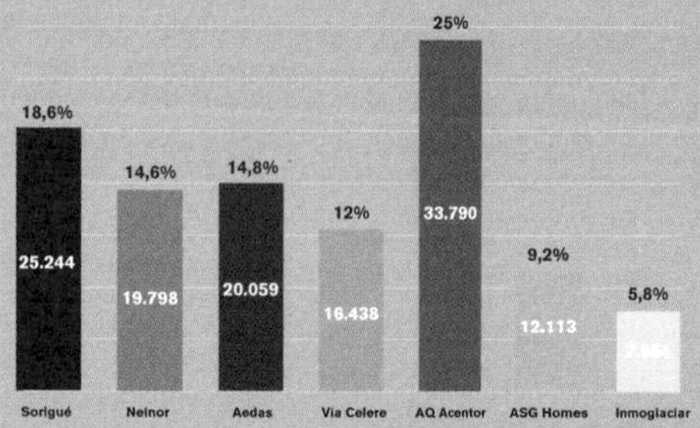

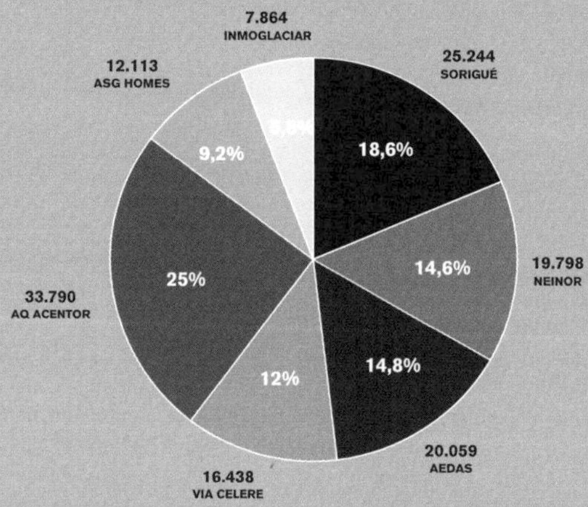

Then, obviously, there is our team who are in constant evolution and growth, always with the will to learn and contribute to the studio with their talent. Among all of them we would like to make a special mention to Georgina Morales, director of the office and alma mater of it. Also, we cannot forget to mention Saúl Ajuria, Claudia Antonacci, Javier Bernal, Estel.la Bosch, Byron Cadena, Aude Croiset, Mario Espinoza, Jordi Farell, Carlos García-Sancho, Ricard Gonzalvo, Luka Kreze, Maciek Lastowski,

Nico Millán, Anaïs Millot, Albert Montilla, Linda Penkhues, Elena Roland, Ernest Ruiz, Joan S. Sorrondegui, Luciana Teodozio and many others who have enabled us to make countless projects through all these years.

We have worked alongside our collaborators. The world of building and architecture encompasses numerous aspects which go beyond design. To make projects posible, a great deal of specialists from different sectors (structures, installations, interior design, bio-architecture, sustainability, energetic efficiency, budgets, acoustics, etc.) are required. Without them our work would not be posible. We have always tried to surround ourselves with companies and people who, as us, are willing to evolve, innovating and upgrading the processes. All this time we have counted on the knowledge and experience of professionals such as Ramón Presta, Daniel Guzmán, Josep Grau, Ferran Figuerola, Álex Sasplugas, Xavier Badia, Miquel Rodríguez, Javier Fernández, José Antonio Molina, Oriol Giménez, Jordi Noguera, Pere Ollé, Mauro Manca, Giorgia Conti, Javier de Lemus, Guillem Baraut, Xavier Pallàs, Vicens García, etc.

Equally important is the role of those who help us to picture our works, before even having them built, through 3D visualization, or after through video and photography. These artists are essential and play a fundamental role in our career. People such as Marc Albiol, Mario Echigo, Marc Canut or Albert Marín have created most of the visual images of this book. And others like Lluís Ros or Adrià Goula have captured the essence of our works through photography.

Communicating is as important as visualizing. There are hundreds of documents, presentations, conferences, events, contests, websites, publications. Etc. which we have created and in which we have participated in order to spread our work and to transmit our ideas. All these would not be possible without design and communication experts. People like Natalia Cambello, Pati Núñez or Tomoko Sakamoto who have enabled the diffusion of our work.

Communication plays a very important role in conceptualizing and visualizing our ideas.

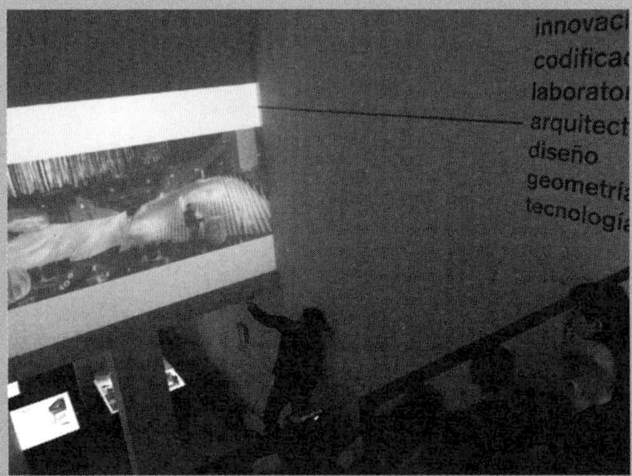

Friday's On-a talks serve as an inspiration to to undertake our daily challenges.

Following the lines of continuous investigation and training, we have been inviting many people from the architecture, arts, design and engineering fields, every Friday, to our ON-A talks. These were informal chats, on-site and virtual, which have served of great inspiration and motivation to our studio. We are talking about distinguished professionals such as Emma Bellosta, Arian Hakimi, Júlia Gallardo, Javier Villar, Riccardo La Magna, Carmelo Zappulla, Pablo Ros, Matteo Loma, Jonathan Fernández, Sheila Llovet, Anna Torndelacreu, Arturo Fernández, Joan Tarrús, Francesc Gómez, Javier Fúrquez, Aitor Pinilla, Ewald Jooste, Tomás Guyot, Paul Cureton, Candela de Bortoli and many others. Thank you for enlightening us with your knowledge and experience.

Lastly, we would like to thank our family and friends. The ones who are here, the ones who have left us and the ones to come. Many thanks for everything, Trini and Isabel.

LEAN2CRADLE
CONSTRUCÍA

EL ÉXITO DE UNA BUENA GESTIÓN
Emma Bellosta

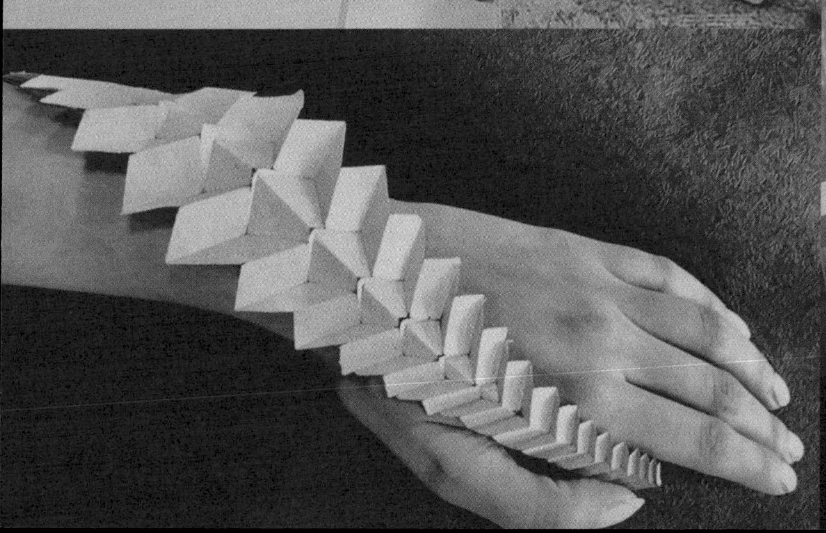

ON-A
Innovation-Architecture
Design, Sustainability, Emotion, Technology

Published by
Actar Publishers, New York, Barcelona
www.actar.com

Authors
ON-A
Eduardo Gutiérrez, Jordi Fernández

Edited by
Ricardo Devesa

Graphic Design
Actar, ON-A

Translation, copy editing and proofreading
Angela K. Bunning

ON-A editorial coordination
Natalia Cambello

ON-A drawings coordination
Luciana Teodózio

Printing and binding
Arlequin & Pierrot

Distribution
Actar D, Inc. New York, Barcelona.

New York
440 Park Avenue South, 17th Floor
New York, NY 10016, USA
salesnewyork@actar-d.com

Barcelona
Roca i Batlle 2
08023 Barcelona, Spain
eurosales@actar-d.com

Indexing
English ISBN: 978-1-948765-68-8
Library of Congress Control Number: 2020947164

Printed in Europe

Publication date: December 2021